NORTH LONDON

ARSENAL

PATRICK VIEIRA

Emirates
FLY BETTER

Fly Emirate

Dreamcast

Arsenal

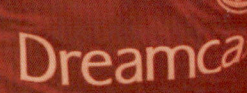

Dreamcas

AFC

ARSENAL
LEGENDS

Written by Adrian Besley

sona
BOOKS

sona
BOOKS

© Danann Publishing Limited 2025

First published in the UK by Sona Books, an imprint of Danann Media Publishing Limited

CAT NO: SON0679

The publishers would like to thank the following sources for their kind
permission to reproduce the pictures in this book.

Getty images:

Ben Radford	Jim Watson	Universal Images Group
Gary Prior	Phil Cole	Arsenal FC via Getty Images
Alex Livesey	Richard Heathcote	Simon Wilkinson
Allsport UK	David Cannon	Icon Sport via Getty Images
Mark Thompson	Shaun Botterill	AFP via Getty Images
Mike Hewitt	Ferdaus Shamim	Mark Leech
Dennis Oulds	Stuart MacFarlane	Offside via Getty Images

All other images: Alamy and Wiki Commons

Book design: Kevin Gardner

Cover design: Darren Grice

Project editor: Martin Corteel

Proof reader: Sofia Della Valle

Printed in EU.

ISBN: 978-1-915343-84-0

CONTENTS

INTRODUCTION

Arsenal are the biggest and most successful club in London. Their Emirates Stadium has over 60,000 fans singing their hearts out at every match, while millions more follow their progress on every continent around the world. They have amassed such a devoted following for their history of success over nearly 100 years, for their great players and the iconic teams that have worn the red and white and for the incredible games the club has played in down the years.

Arsenal have been champions of England on 13 occasions and have won the FA Cup 14 times (more than any other club). Their history is full of passion and glory; stylish destructions of opponents, hard fought battles and on several occasions the most unlikely of triumphs against all odds. These are great teams not only of Arsenal but of English football itself; they are

the club which dominated the 1930s, won the double in the 1970s, came back to the top twenty years later and in the early 21st century played some of the best football on the planet.

Arsenal's magnificent tradition is built on the club's legends; the players who have led or starred in those great sides. This book spotlights the contributions of the most prolific goalscorers, greatest goalkeepers and the inspirational captains who lit up the Arsenal Stadium at Highbury or Emirates Stadium. It features each era's heroes from Alex James to Liam Brady; Tony Adams to Thierry Henry and Ian Wright to Bukayo Saka, as well as fans' favourites such as David Rocastle, Martin Ødegaard and Freddie Ljungburg.

The architects of those great teams have not been forgotten either. Forging a team from youth prodigies, unsung heroes and expensive signings, the club's great managers have added their own character to the club's identity. Herbert Chapman, Bertie Mee and Arsène Wenger are Arsenal legends too, and the book pays tribute to their and other great manager's contributions.

In the following pages we feature Arsenal's greatest and never-to-be-forgotten players, matches, teams and managers in a celebration of the club's glittering and exhilarating history. These are the legends of Arsenal Football Club.

▼ Arsenal moved into the Emirates stadium in 2006, after having spent 93 years at their previous home Highbury

ARSENAL LEGENDS

H ere are the ten greatest Arsenal's players of all time — the true legends. Some of them are universally acknowledged heroes of the club, but others might be up for discussion. How do you assess the contributions of defenders versus strikers? Is it harder to reach the heights if your team is struggling? And can you really compare players of different eras? Everyone will have their own view on this top ten — read on to see if you agree!

▶ Gunners fans enjoying the spectacle of watching their favourite team at Emirates Stadium

THIERRY HENRY

Arsenal's top legend is the club's all-time record goalscorer Thierry Henry, the focal point of Arsène Wenger's superb team and one of the Premier League's greatest ever players. He epitomised a team of class and style, and he was not only a peerless goalscorer, but also a creator of goals for his teammates, and remains Arsenal through and through.

▶ Thierry Henry in full flow for Arsenal

▼ Henry savours the atmosphere of Arsenal's last game at Highbury, before their move to Emirates Stadium

377 APPEARANCES
228 GOALS

THIERRY HENRY

13

When Thierry Henry first stepped onto the pitch for Arsenal in August 1999, few could have predicted the seismic impact he would have on both the club and English football. Over the next eight years, Henry would not only become Arsenal's all-time leading goal scorer, but he would also redefine the role of a modern striker and leave a legacy that is part of the club's identity to this day.

Having had an unhappy six months at Juventus, Henry signed for £11 million four days before his 22nd birthday. He was certainly talented and had electric pace, but his time in Italy had raised questions over his ability to adapt to top-level football. Arsène Wenger had no such doubts. He had coached Henry when they were at Monaco together and gave the teenager his debut.

Although he had previously played him as a left-winger, Wenger had always envisaged Henry maturing into a striker. That was the Wenger way — to reposition and transform a player — and now seemed

▲ After scoring against Derby County, goal celebrations for Henry with Dennis Bergkamp in 1999

the ideal time to enact the plan. However, when Henry failed to score in his first eight games for the club, the Highbury faithful were not quite so sure. Wenger held his nerve, though, and Henry finally found the net as a late substitute in a game against Southampton with a curling effort from outside the box. Even that wasn't the turning point. That came two months later against Derby County when Henry switched the game around with two classic and stylish finishes. It was an impressive performance and he left the field to a standing ovation. He scored 26 goals that season, becoming especially lethal in its last two months, scoring in 10 consecutive matches and destroying Chelsea with a scintillating display and two goals.

After playing a major role in France's Euro

2000 triumph, Henry made himself at home in the Premier League. He was Arsenal's top goalscorer in the 2000-01 season with 22 goals in 53 appearances, including a virtuoso performance against Manchester United in which his winning goal, a flick with his back to goal on the edge of the area followed by a swivel and a scintillating volley, was simply stunning. On Boxing Day 2000 he scored his first hat-trick for the Gunners in a 6-1 thrashing of Leicester City and, although an FA Cup final defeat meant he was still to win a trophy at the club, that was all about to change.

The season in which Thierry Henry finally emerged as one of the world's best footballers was 2001-02. His unique blend of speed, athleticism, intelligence and technique made him unique: a winger, playmaker, goal-poacher and centre-forward in one lithe, elegant goal-machine. There was nothing he couldn't do. He was a complete attacker, able to stretch defences, link up play and deliver moments of individual brilliance. He picked up his first silverware in Arsenal's Double-winning season, netted 32 goals in all competitions and won the Golden Boot with 24 league goals. And he was only getting started…

From 2002 until 2006, 'Titi', as he was affectionately known, was the best forward in the world. He was Footballer of the Year on three occasions and was a Ballon d'Or runner-up in 2003 (and third in 2004). He was the Premier League top scorer in four of the five seasons, twice won the European Golden Shoe (the first player to officially win the award twice in a row) and was Arsenal player of the year from 2003 to 2005. In 2003-04 he joined a select group of 10 strikers who have hit 30 goals or more in a single Premier League season.

So many of his goals in those golden years were to savour. When he put on the turbos, his pace was

▲ Thierry Henry battles for the ball with Manchester United's Mikaël Silvestre, October 2000

extraordinary (Jamie Carragher has said it was like chasing someone on a motorbike) and his ability to finish was just incredible. His signature side-foot diagonally across the keeper judged the angle to perfection time and time again, and every now and then he would produce something that left even rival fans open-mouthed. His lightening solo run from his own half against Tottenham in November 2002, when he dummied and shimmied his way past three defenders before planting the ball in the very corner of the net, is many Gooners' favourite. Then there is the second of his hat-tricks against Liverpool in April 2004, when he ran at a fully manned, white-shirted wall, slaloming through two lines of defenders, before executing the coolest of finishes. Or, for pure

impudence, the moment against Charlton Athletic in October 2024 when, with his back to goal in the six yard box, he sent a genius back-heel through the defenders' legs and into the far corner.

What set Henry apart from other strikers was that he was not just a fantastic goalscorer, but also a goal creator. Wenger is on record as saying that, 'None of the great goalscorers in history can compare with his assist record.' He was right. Henry reinvented the role of the striker. He thrived in Wenger's fluid 4-4-2 or 4-2-3-1 systems, often dropping deep or drifting wide to create space. His teammates Robert Pires, Dennis Bergkamp and Freddie Ljungberg were world-class strikers, too, but Henry was crucial in creating chances for them. He made as many goals as he scored and consistently led the league in assists, even though he rarely took a corner and his free-kicks were direct shots on goal. He made 154 goal contributions over those four seasons, most successfully in the 2002—03 season, when he registered 20 assists alongside his 24 goals — still a Premier League record. In his career at Arsenal he made 93 assists, second only to Dennis

◀ In full charge against Tottenham, 2002

▼ Scoring the first goal for Arsenal v Inter Milan at the San Siro Stadium, Italy. The Gunners were playing a Champions League Group B game in November 2003

Bergkamp in the history of the club.

In those years, Thierry Henry's goals and assists kept the trophies coming at Highbury. After the 2001-02 Double, he was part of the team that won the title in 2003-04 and the FA Cup in both 2002-03 and 2004-05 (though he was injured for the final). Unfortunately, he was never to collect a European trophy, despite playing some of his best matches in Arsenal's continental adventures. He does, however, hold the club record for most appearances in European competitions (89) and is also the club's leading goalscorer in Europe with 42 goals.

He struck twice when Arsenal thrashed Inter Milan 5-1 at the San Siro and hit a hat-trick in Roma, capped by a brilliant shot from a free-kick, but two of

his European goals will never be forgotten. First, in October 2005, having missed six weeks through injury, he came back to play at Sparta Prague. He equalled Ian Wright's Arsenal goalscoring record of 185 goals with a sublime curling shot, before breaking it with a second strike. Then, later in that Champions League run, his performance and goal in the defeat of Real Madrid's Galacticos at the Bernabéu went down in Arsenal history.

After the departure of Patrick Vieira in the summer of 2005, Henry was appointed Arsenal captain. It was a season when he scored his 100th league goal at Highbury, became the club's

◀ In his time at Arsenal, Thierry Henry developed into the perfect striker

▼ After playing his last game for Arsenal, Henry shows his appreciation to the Arsenal fans

leading scorer ever and, on the final day of the season, scored a hat-trick against Wigan Athletic in the last ever match played at Highbury, completing the season as the league's top goalscorer. He led the team out in the Champions League final in Paris and provided the cross for Sol Campbell's goal, but was unable to bring the trophy back to London.

After an injury-hit season, Arsenal's first at the Emirates Stadium, Thierry Henry left for Barcelona in a £20 million transfer in June 2007. There he would collect a Champions League winners' medal and win La Liga twice in three seasons. In 2010 he moved to play for the New York Bulls, but in January 2012, nearly five years after leaving the club, he made a surprise return to Arsenal. With the Gunners' striker Gervinho away at the Africa Cup of Nations, he came back for two months as cover. Donning the number 12 shirt instead of his iconic 14, he scored the winner as a substitute against Leeds United in the FA Cup third round. Having curled the ball into the bottom corner

with his right foot, his familiar celebration — arms wide with a serene expression — made it look as if he had never left. He made four appearances, scoring three times, including in his last Premier League game, a stoppage time strike to beat Sunderland.

Thierry Henry is celebrated with a statue outside Emirates Stadium, frozen mid-celebration from his famous knee-slide against Spurs. He was not just the Gunners' greatest ever goalscorer, but epitomised the club's modern identity: expressive and razor-sharp, cool and stylish. His record of 228 goals for Arsenal may one day be beaten, but what he achieved and brought to the club will never be forgotten. There was, and probably never will be, anyone quite like him.

▼ After a remarkable career at Arsenal, a statue of Henry in classic pose sits outside Emirates Stadium in his honour. It was unveiled to the public in December 2011

DENNIS BERGKAMP

BERGKAMP

ONE OF THE GREATEST PLAYERS OF HIS GENERATION

A true Arsenal legend, Dennis Bergkamp spent 11 glorious seasons in North London. He is generally held to be one of the greatest players of his generation as well as one of Arsenal's greatest ever players, and won a cabinet full of major trophies with the club, plus a shelf full of individual awards.

▶ Dutch master, Dennis Bergkamp

▼ The Bergkamp statue at the Emirates Stadium features a pose inspired by his legendary goal against Newcastle in 2003

423 APPEARANCES
120 GOALS

◀ Arsenal Manager Bruce Rioch signed Dennis Bergkamp from Inter Milan and unveiled the striker in August 1995

▼ Bergkamp smashes the ball past Leicester keeper Kasey Keller to hammer home his first hat-trick for the Gunners

inconsiderable success for Ajax. In 1989-90 the club won the Eredivisie for the first time in five years, and Bergkamp was top scorer in 1991, 1992 and 1993, as well as Dutch Footballer of the Year in 1992 and 1993. This earned him a 1990 call-up to the national side and at Euro 1992 he scored three as the Dutch reach the tournament semi-finals. Exposure on the international stage led to interest from

Any Arsenal fan can probably tell you three things about Dennis Bergkamp. Number one, he was named after Scotland and Manchester United super-striker Denis Law, although the second 'n' had to be added to satisfy the Dutch registrar. Number two, he is phobic about flying — he was jokingly known as the 'Non-flying Dutchman', which made European away fixtures and travelling with Holland's national team quite tricky. And number three, he was simply one of the most talented and skilful players ever to pull on the shirt.

Born in 1969 in the Dutch capital, Amsterdam, at the age of 11 Bergkamp was spotted by an Ajax scout. His boyhood footballing heroes were Glenn Hoddle, whose control and precision he admired, and Johan Cruyff, also long-associated with Ajax. In fact, when he was 12 he was lucky enough to be briefly coached by the master and when he made his professional debut at 17, in December 1986, it was Cruyff, then managing Ajax, who gave him his chance.

Within a couple of seasons he had established himself as a regular first-team player in a period of not several European clubs and in 1993 he left Ajax for Inter Milan, after 239 appearances and 122 goals for his home club.

Having initially played as a wide midfielder, as a teenager Bergkamp was moved to principal striker and then second striker, where he found he was more comfortable, more effective and where he stayed for the rest of his career. However, that career took something of a nosedive in Italy, where he never quite seemed to fit in, as a player and as a personality — he came across as reserved whereas the Italian fans expected exuberance. He was plagued by minor injuries and fatigue, particularly after the 1994 World Cup, where he was the lynchpin of a Netherlands side that got as far as the quarter-finals.

After two frankly disappointing seasons at Inter, in 1995 Bergkamp moved to Arsenal,

where he found not only renewed focus, but a legion of fans who truly appreciated the way he played. Although very much associated with the Wenger era, Bergkamp was actually signed to Arsenal by Bruce Rioch, who had a short spell managing Arsenal in the mid-90s, after George Graham was sacked under a cloud for taking 'bungs'. The transfer fee was £2.5 million — a club record at the time — but the Dutchman wasn't exactly an overnight success, taking time to settle in to the Premier League and scoring only a modest 11 goals in 33 appearances in his first season.

However, when Arsène Wenger arrived at Highbury in September 1996 he recognised that Bergkamp was well suited to the type of attacking football he wanted to play and that he could build his team around his remarkable talent. Mind you, in Wenger's first season in charge, 1996-97, Bergkamp had another low total, scoring just 12 goals in 29 league games, but he was nonetheless highly influential and made 13 important assists, including setting up Tony Adams to volley in the 88th-minute winner against Tottenham Hotspur in November 1996 (he also scored in his own right in injury time).

The following season, though, saw Arsenal top the 1997-98 Premier League and lift the FA Cup, with Bergkamp absolutely key to both achievements, even though unfortunately he had to miss the Cup final itself due to a hamstring injury. He was also top scorer with 22 goals and that tally included his favourite strike for Arsenal: the third of his first hat-trick for the club, away to Leicester.

The following year, Manchester United put Arsenal out of the FA Cup in a semi-final replay, but it was a tight game. At 1-1 with injury time imminent, Phil Neville brought down Ray Parlour and Arsenal were awarded the penalty. Bergkamp stepped up to take it, but the shot was saved by stalwart United keeper Peter Schmeichel. Ryan Giggs got the eventual winner for United in extra time (incidentally, a goal that is generally acknowledged as one of the best FA Cup goals of all time) and Bergkamp never took another penalty.

◀ Bergkamp celebrates scoring against Deportivo in the UEFA Cup, with teammates Emmanuel Petit and Davor Šuker, March 2000

The Gunners also lost the 1998-99 league title, again to Manchester United, on the final day of the season, but despite all that it was a pretty good year for Bergkamp. He managed 12 Premier goals and 13 assists in 29 appearances and 16 goals from 40 appearances overall, making him the club's second top scorer, behind Frenchman Nicolas Anelka.

Arsenal came second in the league to United once more in 1999-2000, although instead of losing the title by a single point, this time they trailed Alex Ferguson's side by a somewhat embarrassing 18 points. They had gone out of the FA Cup early on, in a fourth round replay at Leicester City's Filbert Street ground. That was in January, right at the start of the new millennium, and they were already out of the League Cup and the Champions League, so that left just the UEFA Cup to focus on.

To accommodate larger crowds, for the last couple of years Arsenal had been playing European home fixtures at Wembley, but for the UEFA Cup they switched back to Highbury. Bergkamp scored against Nantes, Deportivo La Coruña and Lens — the goal in the latter game was particularly stylish — as the team progressed to the final, where they met the Turkish side Galatasaray in Copenhagen. The two were fairly well matched and both had chances, so it went to golden goal extra time and then penalties. Patrick Vieira's shot hit the crossbar and Galatasaray emerged the ultimate victors, but Bergkamp could only watch as he had been substituted in the 75th minute.

In December 2000 Bergkamp agreed to extend his contract at Arsenal, but in 2000-01 the club came second in the league for the third year running, again to Manchester United, although this time the margin was reduced to a 'mere' 10 points. In the FA Cup, Arsenal reached the final, but lost 2-1 to Liverpool and Bergkamp only came on as a sub in the 90th minute — he had been somewhat sidelined by the emergence of Thierry

Henry and Sylvain Wiltord as the principal strikers.

Wenger's second Double came in 2001-02. Victory over Manchester United in the season's penultimate game secured the league title and a 2-0 win over

◀ Lifting the Premiership title after Arsenal were left undefeated in the 2003-04 season

◀ Bergkamp holds off a challenge from FC Thun's Selver Hodžić to score in their Champions League tie, 2005

scoring his hundredth goal for the club during the cup campaign. In 2003-04, though, Arsenal topped the final table once again and in the process became the first team in over a hundred years to be unbeaten in the league for a whole season — this was the era of the 'Invincibles'.

As 2004-05 rolled by, Arsenal failed again to defend their league title, ultimately finishing second to Chelsea, but the final home match of the season was particularly memorable for Bergkamp as he scored one and provided three assists in a 7-0 victory over Everton. Unsurprisingly, he was made man of the match. Thierry Henry was injured and Bergkamp began the FA Cup final, against Manchester United, playing as a lone striker, but was substituted before extra time. Arsenal eventually won on penalties.

Bergkamp's last season at Arsenal was also Arsenal's last season at the old Highbury ground and 15 April 2006 was designated Dennis Bergkamp Day, when his contributions to the club's achievements were celebrated. He came on as a sub against West Brom and not only set up Robert Pires' strike, but in the 89th minute scored himself. That proved to be his last goal in competitive football for Arsenal, although the first match at the new Emirates stadium was his testimonial, against his former club Ajax.

What made Dennis Bergkamp a legend? He was pure class. He had an ability to control the ball with a single touch and flick it on, accurately and apparently effortlessly. The consummate playmaker, his fluid movement made him hard to mark, he had excellent powers of concentration and could read the game with ease. He was a joy to watch, deeply serious about football and undoubtedly one of the most outstanding players to wear number 10.

Chelsea enabled them to lift the FA Cup. In league and Cup games Bergkamp made 39 appearances and scored 12 goals, including a winning header in the fourth round of the FA Cup against Liverpool. However, as always, his assists added up and he was given 12 in the league.

In 2002-03 Arsenal failed to retain the league title, but did lift the FA Cup once more, with Bergkamp

TONY ADAMS

AN ICONIC FIGURE IN THE HISTORY OF THE CLUB

A one-club man, a title-winner in three different decades, a double-Double winner, the Gunners' most successful captain ever and one of a select few to have a statue of them erected at Emirates Stadium — Tony Adams spent 19 years in red and white, and was, and surely remains, the one and only 'Mr Arsenal'.

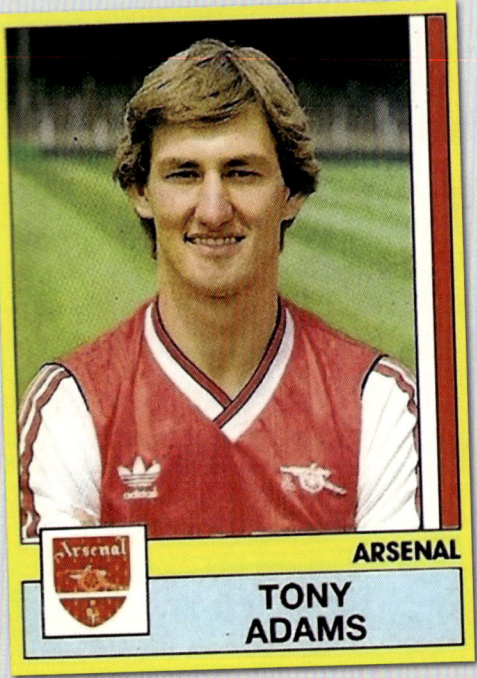

ARSENAL

TONY ADAMS

▶ 'Mr Arsenal', Tony Adams

◀ Tony Adams trading card

669 APPEARANCES
48 GOALS

TONY ADAMS

An Essex County Schools player, Tony Adams was signed by Arsenal as a 13-year-old in 1980. Having established himself at England under-17 level, he was given an apprentice contract by Terry Neill in 1983. In November of that year, weeks after his 17th birthday, he made his debut in a home defeat by Sunderland. In a difficult season for the club only made respectable by a late run after Don Howe replaced Neill, he made two other appearances. Those were dark times for Arsenal fans and the emergence of a promising, homegrown young defender was one of the few bright spots on the horizon.

The following campaign saw Adams, who was now 18, play in 16 matches. He was preferred to his fellow England youth international Martin Keown as a partner for David O'Leary, and the Irishman would serve as a great mentor and role model for the ever-improving youngster. Adams' breakthrough season, though, came in 1986-87. New manager George Graham had refreshed the squad and, along with other young players such as Michael Thomas, David Rocastle, Niall Quinn and Martin Hayes, he delivered Arsenal's first trophy for eight years, the League Cup. Adams' contribution was recognised by the presentation of the PFA Young Player of the Year award and a debut for his country as the first player to represent England who had been born after the national team's 1966 World Cup triumph.

At the age of just 21, Adams was appointed captain by Graham. Described by his manager as, 'My sergeant-major on the pitch — a colossus,' he was Arsenal's youngest ever captain and would wear the armband proudly for the next 14 years. Graham's gameplan relied on a watertight defence and Adams led the legendary back four — Dixon, Winterburn, Adams, Bould — a unit so disciplined and reliable that they became the best English football had ever seen.

Wearing the number 6 shirt with which he would become synonymous, Adams lifted the (old) First Division trophy twice in three seasons. First in 1988 after the sensational win at Anfield and then in 1990,

◀ A young Tony Adams in 1984

▶ Adams celebrates clinching the 1988-89 First Division title at Anfield with (left to right): Martin Hayes, Lee Dixon, and John Lukic

when he led a team that only conceded 18 goals all season. He was a tremendous defender who read the game superbly, timed his tackles to perfection and was dominant in the air — in either penalty area. He was quick on his feet and deceptively strong. He stood firm against bigger forwards and was never one to back away from a fight. He was also a natural leader. As captain, Adams would galvanise the whole team for battle and even from an early age he had no qualms about calling out more experienced teammates if he felt they were not giving their all on the pitch. His will to win was infectious and instilled a fight-to-the-end spirit in the whole team.

However, from the mid-1980s Adams became increasingly dependent on alcohol. He has said he was an alcoholic for 12 years and, remarkably, played while intoxicated on a few occasions (once, he has claimed, receiving the man of the match award). He spent four months in prison in 1990 after crashing his car while drunk, but did not become a recovering alcoholic until 1996. Despite this addiction, he played over 40 matches in most seasons and, despite the prison sentence, still managed to make 30 league appearances in the title-winning 1990-91 season. It is telling that Arsenal's only league defeat of that campaign came against Chelsea while Adams was behind bars.

Although feted by Arsenal players, staff and fans for his performances in the early 1990s, he often failed to earn the recognition he deserved. Sections of the media persevered with their vindictive 'donkey' label

for too long, while England managers Bobby Robson and Graham Taylor both looked elsewhere for a central defender. Nevertheless, Adams was playing some of the best football of his life. In 1992-93, he was integral to Arsenal's unique capture of both cups. In the FA Cup, he scored in the quarter-final, heading home a Merson free-kick for an equaliser against Ipswich despite a head dressing. Then in the semi-final at Wembley, with ten minutes remaining in the match, the same combination contrived a winner against Tottenham Hotspur, with the skipper rising at the far post to nod home.

In the following season, Adams played some of his greatest games in an Arsenal shirt in the run to the Cup-Winners' Cup final. In a tough quarter-final against a quality Turin side he led a masterclass in defending in Italy and then scored the winner in the second leg at Highbury with another far post header from a free-kick. In the semi-final against a PSG team that included David Ginola and George Weah, and in the final against a technically superior Parma, he was a giant, leading Arsenal to their first European trophy for 24 years. There certainly was no argument about him collecting Arsenal's player of the season award.

By 1995 George Graham's tenure as manager at Arsenal was coming to an end, but Tony Adams remained his rock in the centre of defence. He once again shepherded his team to the Cup-Winners' Cup final, even stepping up to take the fourth penalty in the semi-final shoot-out against Sampdoria. Showing no nerves he blasted his effort and nearly split the net. Unfortunately, he was injured when Arsenal were defeated in the final in Paris.

Adams had a great summer in 1996. Terry Venables

had brought him back into the England set-up and he was captain for their famous run to the semi-finals of the Euros. He had also finally confronted his alcoholism and had been sober for six weeks when Arsène Wenger arrived at the club. He had initial reservations about the Frenchman's ability to adapt to English football, but was willing to give him a chance. He soon discovered that Wenger's tactics would free him up to play a more expansive game. For once, Adams

was bringing the ball out of defence, venturing upfield and even getting into scoring positions. In a 3-1 win over Tottenham just six games into Wenger's reign, he scored the vital second goal after finding himself running onto a sublime flick by Dennis Bergkamp to strike a half-volley from a tight angle.

Wenger later referred to the defence he inherited

▲ A delighted Adams after the Gunners beat Sheffield Wednesday at Wembley in May 1993

◄ Captain Tony Adams leads out Arsenal at Highbury

TONY ADAMS

as 'graduates in the art of defending' and honoured the now 30-year-old Adams as a 'Doctor of Defence'. He had faith in that back four, but also knew he could trust his captain to play on the left or right depending on his partner. Adams missed ten league games in the 1996-97 season, but his contribution was reflected in the fact he was still named in the PFA Team of the Year.

Although now more prone to injury, Adams still managed to play around 35 matches in each of the following four seasons as Wenger's teams hit heights never witnessed before. He was the mainstay of the 1997-98 Double-winning team, although his most memorable moment was scoring the fourth goal in the 4-0 win over Everton that secured the league title. When Steve Bould played a Bergkamp-esque through ball to the captain, who blasted it in from a centre-forward position, it was the perfect end to a perfect season for the disbelieving and ecstatic fans.

As the new manager brought in new players, it was the captain who kept them organised on the field and disciplined in their defensive duties. For an ageing player, Adams was playing as well as ever. Despite losing the captaincy to Alan Shearer, he kept his place in the England team for the 1998 World Cup and then captained them in the 2000 Euros, becoming the first, and still only, player to make tournament appearances for England in three separate decades. In January 2001, having made 66 appearances, Adams retired

from international football in order to prolong his Arsenal career.

He played 38 games for the club that season, but a knee injury, the worst of his career, limited his appearances in the 2001-02 campaign. Nevertheless, he was still captain and was an inspirational presence throughout. 'He brings so much hunger into the dressing room,' said Thierry Henry of his captain. 'He prepares you to go out and fight.' Adams lifted the FA Cup after playing in the victory over Chelsea in the final and, despite being sidelined, raised the Premier League trophy at Highbury in the last match of the season; his final official match for the club before retirement.

A sell-out 38,000 attended his testimonial against Celtic at Highbury in May 2002 and chanted in vain for 'one more year'. Tony Adams honours list shows the part his leadership played in a fabulous era in the club's history: four league titles, three FA Cups, two Doubles, a League Cup and a Cup-Winners' Cup. Only David O'Leary played more games for the Gunners and Mr Arsenal will forever be an iconic figure in the history of the club.

◄ Celebrating in style, his goal against Everton May in 1998

▼ Adams was immortalised as a statue in 2011, outside the North Bank at Emirates Stadium with a familiar pose

IAN WRIGHT

THE CLUB'S TOP SCORER FOR SIX SEASONS IN A ROW

Wrighty had it all. A striker's nose for goal, bags of talent, a determined streak and oodles of charisma. The club's top scorer for six seasons in a row and their all-time leading scorer at that time, he bridged George Graham's domestic cup Double winners and Arsène Wenger's league and cup Double winning sides.

▶ Ready to pounce on goal, Ian Wright

▼ Wrighty with his Golden Boot award for the 1991-92 season with the Gunners

288 APPEARANCES
185 GOALS

'Ian Wright, Wright, Wright! Ian Wright, Wright, Wright!' The chant that rang out from the North Bank was simple, but, not unlike the player himself, got straight to the point. 'Wrighty' had a personality the size of a house and after seven seasons at Arsenal established himself as a never-to-be-forgotten hero and the man who finally broke Cliff Bastin's club goalscoring record. He was undoubtedly one of the greats, but, nearly overlooked as a professional footballer in his youth, was eternally grateful and played like it.

Born in Woolwich, South East London, just like the club itself, nothing came easy to the young Ian Wright. Brought up in poverty by his mother and an abusive father, unable to win a professional contract despite trials at Southend United and Brighton and Hove Albion, he even spent a few days in prison for unpaid motoring fines. But Wrighty always had football to soothe him, playing for his local Sunday league club until the age of 21. In 1985, he got his first break — a contract with non-league Greenwich Borough and after

just a handful of games was spotted by a scout from Crystal Palace.

Before Ian Wright moved to Arsenal, he played for Crystal Palace, having been signed at 22 by Steve Coppell, manager of the (old) Division Two club. He scored nine times as a super-sub in his first season, before forming a partnership with fellow forward Mark Bright and scoring 27 goals as the team won promotion to the top tier. His first season in Division One was limited by injury, but he nonetheless maintained a good strike rate. Famously, recovering from injury, he was a late sub in the 1990 FA Cup final. He scored the equaliser against Manchester United just few minutes after coming onto the field, then put Palace ahead in extra time. He became the Eagles' post-war record goalscorer with 117 goals and was later named as their player of the century.

Wright had already scored five goals in the first eight games of the 1991-92 season before George Graham swept to sign him for a club record fee of £2.5 million.

◄ Ian Wright certainly made an immediate impact at Arsenal, scoring on his league debut against Leicester in 1991

▼ Wrighty wearing his number 8 shirt, in action for the Gunners playing against Crystal Palace in 1993

Arsenal was his destination of choice, boosted by the chance to join up with his childhood friend, David Rocastle (to his great disappointment, Rocky would be sold to Leeds at the end of the season). If fans were wondering whether he was good enough to improve the league champions, he provided an instant answer. He scored with a skidding 18-metre shot right into the

corner on his debut against Leicester City in a League Cup tie and on the following Saturday he registered a hat-trick in his league debut against Southampton. It was incontrovertible: the Gunners had found a new hero.

Arsenal's shaky start to the season had handicapped their title defence, but powered by Wright's goals they climbed the table. By Christmas, he had scored 11 in ten games, including all four in a 4-2 defeat of Everton in December. He was the spearhead of a free-scoring forward line that made a mockery of the 'Boring Arsenal' jibe and his final day repeat hat-trick against Southampton took his Arsenal league tally to 24. To Gooners' delight, the final goal (added to the five he scored at Palace), meant he passed Spurs' Gary Lineker's total to

win the Golden Boot as the league's top scorer. In his first season at the club, he also collected the Arsenal player of the year award.

Wrighty's goalscoring threat proved to be a double-edged sword for the Gunners. He was certainly lethal, with great pace, a fierce shot and a true poacher's intuition for a tap-in. However, that was enough for George Graham to play with even more caution than before. Although Wright formed a good partnership with Alan Smith, Arsenal only scored a meagre 40 league goals in the following season, of which Wright contributed 17.

Arsenal's league form was patchy, but with an emphasis on defence and Wright's ability to nick a goal, the cups were another story. In 1992-93 his strikes powered the Gunners through to win both the League

and FA Cups. In the League Cup he scored a brace in the quarter-finals against Nottingham Forest and in each leg of the semi-final against his old club Crystal Palace. His FA Cup run was even more impressive, beginning with a hat-trick at Yeovil, he had netted eight times by the time they met Sheffield Wednesday in the final. At Wembley, his brilliant jack-knife header opened the scoring in the first tie and in the replay, running clear, his cool finish again put the Gunners ahead.

The following season, 1993-94, he was once again the inspiration behind a cup run, this time the European Cup-Winners' Cup. He scrambled a precious away goal in Odense in the first round and hit two in a scintillating display against Standard Liège in the next. His glancing header helped earn a draw in Paris, but the home leg

◀ Ian Wright leads the Arsenal Wembley joy after victory over Tottenham in the FA Cup semi-final, 1993

▼ Wright battling for the ball when playing Standard Liège in the Cup-Winners' Cup, 1993

against PSG was bittersweet for the striker. Arsenal won through to the final, but a scything tackle after losing the ball led to a yellow card for Wright. It was a second in the competition and enough for him to miss Arsenal's first European trophy since 1970.

As if on a mission, Wright's goals propelled Arsenal to the final of the competition again the next year. He scored in every round on the way to the final, including a sweet curling left-foot shot against Auxerre in the quarter-finals and a flicked header from a corner to give the Gunners a crucial equaliser against Sampdoria in the nail-biting semi-final second leg. Unfortunately, his run came to an end as Arsenal succumbed to Nayim's audacious shot in the final.

By now, Arsenal's number 8 was many fans' favourite player. His goals were the highlights of

◀ Wrighty marked the occasion of beating Cliff Bastin's goal record with his very special t-shirt

▶ Ian Wright proudly displays his Champions League Winners medal in 1998

disappointing league campaigns and the fuel of the cup successes. He had hit over 30 goals in all competitions in three consecutive seasons and such was his reputation that Nike ran the classic advertising line: 'Behind every great goalkeeper there's a ball from Ian Wright.' His solo effort against Everton in 1993, when he tied Matt Jackson in knots before lobbing Neville Southall, is many fans' favourite Wrighty goal, but he could find the net from every kind of finish. Perhaps something that is best demonstrated by his amazing standing chip against Leeds United in 1995, which seemed almost anatomically impossible.

Wright's goal-tally would surely have been even higher if he had not been playing in an ultra-defensive team that struggled for consistency. He then maintained his status as the club's leading goalscorer, despite a public fall-out with Graham's successor, Bruce Rioch, and a promising partnership began with new signing Dennis Bergkamp as the pair netted 39 goals across all competitions.

When Arsène Wenger took over in September 1996, Ian Wright had just scored another hat-trick in a 4-1 defeat of Sheffield Wednesday. His link-up play with Bergkamp (soon to be his away-game roommate) was intuitive and Wrighty scored at the fastest rate in his Arsenal career. At 33 years old he would play 41 times that season and score over 30 goals for the fourth time in Arsenal colours. He was the second-highest Premier League scorer in the 1996-97 season with 23 goals and netted against 17 of Arsenal's 19 opponents, a record (now shared with Van Persie and Salah) for a 20-team Premier League season.

In September 1997, Ian Wright gleefully became Arsenal's greatest ever goalscorer. Bolton Wanderers were the visitors when he equalled Cliff Bastin's 1939 record of 178 goals for the club after 20 minutes. Mistakenly believing he'd broken the record, he revealed a 'Just Done It!' message on his t-shirt. No matter. Five minutes later he struck again and this time really had done it. He then went on to grab yet another hat-trick — the last of the 11 for Arsenal. Despite an injury ruling him out of the second half of the season he still scored 10 league goals in just 24 matches. As a used substitute in the FA Cup final, he was an accredited Double winner — just deserts for someone who had served the club so magnificently over seven seasons. He left aged 34 in July 1998, claiming that being caught by Arsène Wenger while rollerskating along the marble corridors of Highbury had not helped his case!

Wrighty went on to play for West Ham, Nottingham Forest, Burnley and Celtic, and now enjoys a successful media career. He is rightly a Palace hero, but he is an Arsenal legend. In his time at the club they won the Premier League, two FA Cups, a League Cup and a European Cup-Winners' Cup. He also won the First Division Golden Boot in 1991-92, was Arsenal's player of the season in 1991-92 and 1992-93. He is now Arsenal's second highest all-time goalscorer and remains one of the biggest characters ever to play for the club.

IAN WRIGHT

PATRICK VIEIRA

HE HAD A VORACIOUS PASSION FOR WINNING

f any player epitomised the great double
Double-winning and 'Invincible' Arsenal team
it was the tall Frenchman. The man Wenger
chose to kick-start his revolution at Highbury
had the skill to match his physicality. At best he
was both unpassable in defence and unstoppable
charging forward, while his only flaw was a
disciplinary record that reflected his voracious
passion for winning.

▶ Patrick Vieira was an early signing for
Wenger on his arrival at Highbury

◀ Vieira trading card

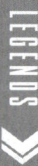

405 APPEARANCES
32 GOALS

When Arsène Wenger arrived at Highbury in September 1996 his first signings were already settling in nicely at the club. Frenchmen Rémi Garde and a leggy 20-year-old named Patrick Vieira had joined in August. Garde proved to be a useful journeyman midfielder, but the six-foot, four-inch Vieira was something else: a once-in-a-career signing, a bargain for just £3.5 million and the foundation upon which the manager would build his revolution at the club.

Born in June 1976, Patrick Vieira had moved to France from Senegal when he was aged eight. He joined AS Cannes when he was 15 years old and within three years was commanding the midfield of the mid-table Ligue 1 team. Despite being made captain, the hot prospect was ambitious and impatient. In 1995, Fabio Capello brought him to AC Milan. His season there is often portrayed as a frustrating time as he played just five first team matches. Vieira himself,

however, didn't view it like that, describing training with Franco Baresi, Paolo Maldini, Marcel Desailly and others as an education and a privilege.

Before Wenger was officially in charge at Arsenal, Vieira had already made his debut for the club as a substitute against Sheffield Wednesday. The Gunners were 1-0 down before he came on, but he made a clear difference. Arsenal won the game 4-1. When Wenger took charge, Vieira had already made himself an automatic first-team choice.

As a central midfielder his physical and technical strength, and his ability to surge forward, was shifting Arsenal from a gritty, defence-based unit to an attacking side. Fans saw enough of the young Frenchman to know that he was one of the main reasons that Wenger's first season was a success. What they didn't realise was how his influence would spur Arsenal to greatness.

◄ Patrick Vieira and Arsène Wenger discuss Arsenal tactics in a match at Fulham

▼ Vieira gets stuck in and wins a crucial tackle against Rory Delap of Southampton in 2002

In summer 1997, Emmanuel Petit was signed from Monaco, with Wenger converting the left-back to a deep-lying defensive midfielder. The two Frenchmen gelled immediately. The newcomer's strength, calmness and passing ability freed Vieira, who was unleashed as a box-to-box phenomenon. Almost unstoppable in full flow, he would stride forward with the ball or make endless lung-bursting runs into space. The Highbury faithful had never seen a midfield partnership that was simultaneously so strong and dangerous.

In that Double-winning season Arsenal only lost twice when the pair were together in the league and FA cup campaigns. Vieira made 46 appearances that season. He made four assists and scored two goals: one a corker in a crucial 3-2 victory over Manchester United when he curled a first-time shot from the edge of the area into the far corner of the net. Such was the impression the pair made that both played in France's midfield at the World Cup. In the final, Vieira played his teammate through to score the home nation's third goal.

In the three trophyless seasons at Arsenal that followed, Vieira missed very few games through injury, but his absence was always noticeable. As each campaign passed, he was exerting increasing influence in the Gunners' play, even when Emmanuel Petit left the club to be replaced by another Frenchman, the tenacious Gilles Grimandi.

The plaudits came thick and fast. Vieira made the PFA Team of the Year every year from 1998 to 2004 and in 2001 he was also named Arsenal's and the Premier League's player of the season. He was a regular for the French team and added a European Championship winner's medal to his collection in 2000. There were some darker moments, though. In 1999 his tired, misplaced pass set up Ryan Giggs for his famous winner in the FA Cup semi-final and his penalty that powered back off the crossbar in the 2000 UEFA Cup final shoot-out contributed to Arsenal's defeat.

There was also his disciplinary record. Vieira's aggressive style of play and intense mentality were a potent mix. Hard tackles, brutal fouls and abusing opposition players and referees all led to him seeing cards. Though he shares a Premier League record of eight red cards, (including being dismissed in the first two games of the 2000-01 season), five were from receiving two yellows. Arsenal fans, of course, loved him even more for being their hard man and positively revelled in his rivalry with Manchester United's Roy Keane.

Vieira's veiled threats to leave the club — he was even rumoured to be going to Manchester United at one point — in the summer of 2001 marked another turning point for him and Arsenal. Sol Campbell joined on a free transfer from Spurs, the club splashed out

▼ Vieira gets to the ball ahead ex-Arsenal player Emmanuel Petit, then of Chelsea in 2003

on a new midfield partner in Giovanni van Bronckhorst and Vieira was made vice-captain. That season was deemed by many to be his best yet in an Arsenal shirt. He played 54 times across all competitions and missed just two Premier League games.

For all that Pires, Henry, Bergkamp and Ljungberg shone in that double-winning season, Vieira was the constant. Game after game he did what he could do better than any midfielder ever: anticipate opposition threats, break up play, win the ball, keep possession, stride upfield and feed those electric forwards. He was a beast: aggressive yet clinical, tall and muscular, but

▼ Roy Keane of Manchester United and Vieira had some interesting encounters that often ended up as heated arguments and fisticuffs

elegant and precise. That Tony Adams shared the honour of lifting the Premier League and FA Cup trophies with his vice-captain showed how much he was valued by the team and the club.

He duly took on the mantle of club captain for the 2002-03 season, revelling in the role and continuing Adams' inspirational leadership style. He drove the team from midfield with his own physical presence and winning mentality, never failing to put in a shift for the

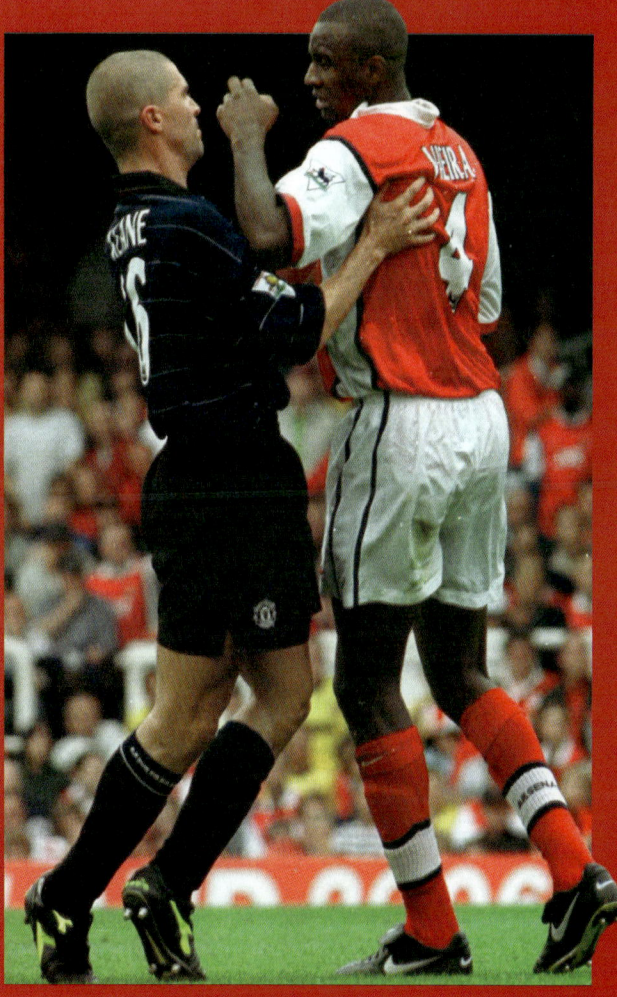

team, even if he sometimes voiced how tired he felt.

The signing of a new defensive midfielder in Gilberto Silva gave him even more freedom. Vieira was the heart and soul of the team that for at least the first half of the season was rated as the best ever seen in English football. His performance against Chelsea in the FA Cup quarter-final was nothing less than magnificent. He played a part in both goals and was masterful in protecting his defence. The fact that they only won the FA Cup that season can be partly attributed to Vieira's absence through injury in vital games in the Premier League run-in.

The captain more than played his part in the title-winning season of 2003-04, yet the first half of the campaign was difficult for Vieira. He was sent off in the bad-tempered encounter at Old Trafford and fined for refusing to leave the pitch. Then a thigh injury led to him missing eight games. While his teammates kept the unbeaten run going, often scrapping for draws, Vieira's return in January sparked a nine-game winning streak. He scored a superb goal after a one-two with Dennis Bergkamp to help beat Chelsea and send the Gunners clear in the league, and he ran the length of the pitch to finish a third-minute opener at White Hart Lane to calm the nerves in their title-winning match. He then capped an historic season with the team's final goal: running on to Bergkamp's pass, rounding the Leicester City keeper and slotting home in style.

The following season, Vieira would record his best Premier League attacking stats in his Arsenal career with six goals and six assists. They included a classic Vieira move at Tottenham, where he won the ball in the centre circle with a strong tackle, muscled past two Spurs players and strode towards goal before calmly stroking the ball past the keeper. He also scored a rare header for Arsenal to take the lead against Manchester United at Old Trafford in February, but defeat there ended title hopes and the captain's tunnel bust-up with Roy Keane captured the headlines. The FA Cup final offered some consolation as Vieira's decisive spot-kick in the shoot-out brought the cup back to Highbury.

That was to be his last kick of the ball for Arsenal. In the summer of 2005, the annual rumours of his departure were finally confirmed as he joined Juventus. Now aged 29, his post-Arsenal career was hampered by regular injuries, but he still performed at a high level, helping Juventus to two titles only to see them rescinded due to a bribery scandal. When Juventus were punished with relegation, he moved to Inter, with whom he won three Serie A titles in four seasons, and finally joined Manchester City for a season, winning an FA Cup medal as an added-time substitute.

One of the greatest midfielders ever, Patrick Vieira shone brightest at Arsenal. He was a founder and integral member of a team that grew to dominate English football; winning three league titles and four FA cups, including two Doubles. He played over 40 matches in all except the first of his nine seasons at the club and was an exemplary captain, leading not only by example, but with passion, encouragement and inspiration.

▲ Patrick Vieira scores the winning penalty for the Gunners in the 2005 FA Cup final against Manchester United

◀ Vieira hoists the Premier League trophy in 2004

ROBERT PIRES

THE MUSKETEER WITH PANACHE AND COOL FINISHING

He was the Invincibles' Musketeer, the left-winger who accomplished the seemingly impossible challenge of improving Wenger's already brilliant team. He is remembered for his panache, his incisive passing and his cool finishing; for his amazing lob over Peter Schmeichel; and for his love of scoring against arch rivals Tottenham Hotspur.

▶ Robert Pires' natural talent shone at Arsenal

▼ A favourite at Highbury, Pires is greeted by fans in the background outside the ground

284 APPEARANCES
84 GOALS

ROBERT PIRES

53

'By the 20th minute I was already thinking, what am I doing here?' Robert Pires was on the bench watching Arsenal at Sunderland in the opening game of the 2000-01 season. When he came on for his debut, the game passed him by. The long balls, tough-tackling and bustle of the English game were not for the silky-skilled newcomer. The season continued in the same vein and many feared that what had seemed an exciting transfer was a damp squib.

The ever-wise Arsène Wenger knew better. He persevered with Pires, who played 51 games that season, and although he continued to struggle, tantalising glimpses of his talent gradually began to

emerge: initially in October, when he ran half the length of the field to equalise against Lazio with only three minutes remaining — enough to progress Arsenal's Champions League campaign; latterly when he scored against Spurs both in the league and in a semi-final FA Cup victory (scoring against the neighbours was a regular habit that he, and Arsenal fans, would come to love), and in the final itself, when his pass for Ljungberg's strike seemed to have won the Cup for Arsenal.

Despite being a French international since 1997, Robert Pires had largely flown under the European radar for much of his early career. He made his name

◄ Finger pointing, Robert Pires scores against old foes Tottenham Hotspur in the FA Cup semi-final, 2001

▼ Pires was initially brought in by Wenger as a replacement for Marc Overmars

play the right-footer on the left wing as a replacement for Marc Overmars.

Only a couple of months of the 2001-02 season had elapsed when those who had branded Pires a luxury player were made to eat their words. His exquisite technique, ability to cut inside from the wing and sublime finishing perfectly blended into a team playing dream football. He was the ideal link between Ashley Cole in defence and Thierry Henry upfront, and Wenger was moved to describe him as 'the oil in the engine'. Through the autumn and winter of that campaign, he had magic in his boots and the Highbury faithful fell head over heels in love.

first at Metz, helping them to a runners-up spot in France's Ligue 1. He then, in 1998, made a big money move to Marseille, who also finished second and were runners-up in the UEFA Cup.

Pires' unhappiness at the club in his second season encouraged Wenger to engineer a similar coup to those that had delivered Vieira and then Henry to Highbury. In 2000, as Real Madrid and Juventus were circling — Pires had just provided the assist for France's Euro 2000 winning goal — the Arsenal boss swooped in and nabbed the 26-year-old for £6 million. Pires had previously played as a number 10 or supporting forward, but the Gunners' boss had a cunning plan to

In the course of that season he scored nine goals in the league and provided 15 assists, more than any other player. Opta rated him the most creative player in the Premiership. A 25-metre shot brought his customary goal at White Hart Lane; a sweetly struck, right-footed volley from the edge of the area led a comeback against Middlesbrough; and, most memorably, in an audaciously skilful goal against Aston Villa he flicked the ball over defender George Boateng before executing the cheekiest of lobs over goalkeeper Peter Schmeichel. 'That's genius. That is genius,' remarked Andy Gray in commentary with Martin Tyler responding: 'A golden goal from a player in a golden shirt, at a golden time for Arsenal.'

His play was so thrilling and integral to the Gunners' free-flowing style that when he tore his cruciate ligament in March many thought Arsenal's title charge might falter. Fortunately, they stayed the course and won the Double. When he tentatively climbed the podium to lift the Premier League trophy, his teammates dropped to their knees and bowed. They knew how valuable his contribution had been. To underline this, despite missing the final two months of the campaign, he was still voted the Football Writers' player of the year and Arsenal's player of the season.

Super Bobby, as the fans called him, was the most stylish looking footballer. His long dark hair, sideburns

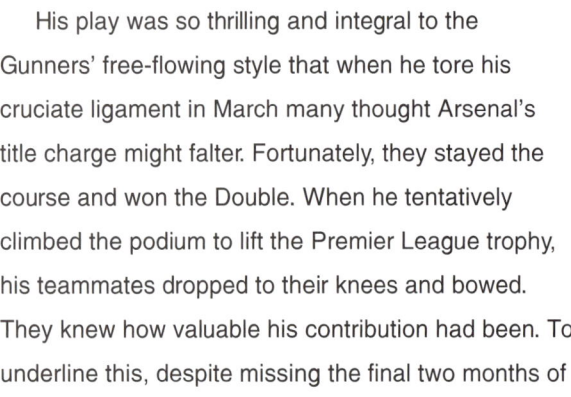

▲ Pires scores for the Gunners when Arsenal met Aston Villa in 2002

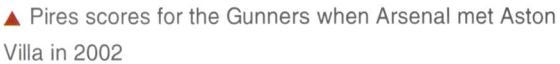

► Praise from the Arsenal team, as they bow and kneel before Pires, who holds up the Premier League trophy in 2002

and goatee cast him perfectly as D'Artagnan, the Musketeer. And he played in a swashbuckling and elegant manner to suit. Although not fast, he was silky smooth and would glide across the pitch. Technically he was faultless, his vision from wide was incredible and his timing with his runs or passes was impeccable. He was a great winger, but also brought in the attributes of a superb number 10. He made chances for others, especially Henry, and had an eye for goal himself — he was the Premier League's top-scoring midfielder for three consecutive seasons — and scored more than

his share of tap-ins from being in the right place at the right time. Not only was he a reliable penalty-taker, but he won plenty, too.

That cruciate injury led to Pires missing the 2002 World Cup with France and the first few months of the new season, and when he came back it seemed he was beginning all over again. He made a few substitute appearances before making his first start in November 2002 against Aston Villa and then it took him just 17 minutes to open his account. In just 21 league games that season he still notched up 14 goals.

He finished the season in style. He hit his first hat-trick for Arsenal in the last home game of the season, against Southampton. It was completed with the most nonchalant, sumptuous curling chip from 30 metres, which lives long in the memory. A week later, he made up for missing the previous year's FA Cup final with the winning goal in Cardiff. Once again Southampton were the victims, but this time he executed a cool, two-touch finish to a marvellous team move which involved Henry, Bergkamp and Ljungberg.

The following season, 2003-04, Pires played an integral part in the legendary 'Invincible' season. He hit the back of the net in the first game of the season and would add another 13 league goals (19 in all competitions). Among them, of course, were strikes home and away against Tottenham, including in the title-winning match, but the most beautiful was a fabulous cut-in from the left and a curling shot from 25-metres which earned a win at Anfield. The performance by an injury-hit team that had just returned from a game in Moscow was a real statement of intent.

Though now in his 30s, Pires' goal tally continued to improve. In 2004-05, he hit chalked up goals in the Premier League, a tally only beaten by Thierry Henry and Crystal Palace's Andrew Johnson. He opened the scoring in the semi-final defeat of Blackburn Rovers with a typical back post tap-in and went on to pick up his second FA Cup winners' medal. He played 100 minutes of the stalemate with Manchester United, but was replaced by Edu before the victorious penalty shoot-out.

Arsenal's final season at Highbury would turn out to be Pires' final season, too. Unfortunately for him, it was not a glorious setting of the sun, but a disappointing, slightly rancorous campaign. His performances did not live up to the extraordinarily high standards he had previously set himself and which had illuminated Highbury for five years.

He found himself left out of the starting 11 and began to feel he had lost the manager's trust. He

did fight his way back into the team and scored 11 goals across all competitions, but he and the team were underperforming. The fiasco in which he and Henry blundered an attempted trick penalty first executed by Johan Cruyff was one of his most memorable contributions. A more positive intervention was his full-bloodied tackle on Patrick Vieira, which led to Henry's goal against Juventus in the Champions League quarter-final, followed by a valiant bolstering of the defence in the semi-final second leg against Villarreal. The final, disappointing for all Arsenal fans, was even more bitter for Pires, who was the unfortunate player to be sacrificed after Jens Lehmann's red card. To this day, he maintains Arsène Wenger was wrong to have substituted him after just 18 minutes.

In the summer of 2006, Pires signed for Valencia. He spent four years at the Spanish club and played over 100 times for them. He then spent a season back in the Premier League with Aston Villa and, despite having retired, turned out for Goa in the inaugural season of the Indian Super League at the age of 40.

His record at Arsenal speaks for itself: two league titles, two FA Cup finals and a Champions League runners-up medal, as well as being named Footballer of the Year in 2002 and making the PFA team of the year for three consecutive seasons from 2001-02. However, many Arsenal fans' memories are less about what he won and more about how he did it: he was a charmer, a great character who was always a delight to watch and one of the most naturally skilful footballers ever to grace the pitch at Highbury.

◀ Holding off the ball from Southampton's Paul Telfer in 2003. Arsenal won the match 6-1 and Pires logged a hat-trick

CESC FÀBREGAS

A FAN FAVOURITE AT THE EMIRATES FROM THE WORD GO

A teenage talent, the like of which had never been seen in English football, Cesc Fàbregas blossomed in Arsène Wenger's team. For eight seasons, his vision, skill and inspirational captaincy made him the envy of rival clubs and a fan favourite in the early years at the Emirates.

▶ Cesc Fàbregas joined the Gunners as a teenager

▼ Fàbregas demonstrating his ability to shake off most players with pace and skill

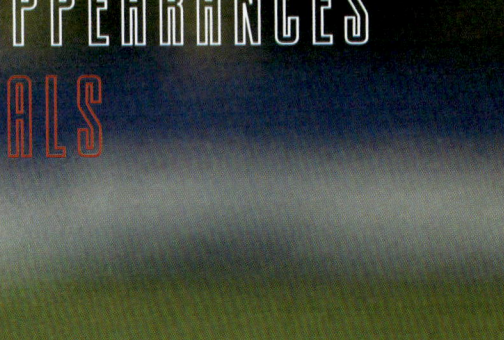

303 APPEARANCES
57 GOALS

From the age of 10, Cesc Fàbregas trained with his local club, Barcelona. Among his teammates were Lionel Messi and Gerard Piqué, and, although he was valued (he was a prolific goalscorer), the young Fàbregas was behind Messi in the pecking order, plus Xavi and Andrés Iniesta were already breaking into the first team. He weighed up his prospects in Spain and, even though it was a bold move for a 16-year-old, decided to move club and country.

In September 2003, shortly after leading Spain to the final of the Under 17 World Cup in Finland, where he was the leading scorer and named the tournament's best player, the young midfielder joined Arsenal. In North London he was the archetypal struggling boy living hundreds of miles from home, but fortunately Arsenal defender Philippe Senderos could speak Spanish and was able to befriend the homesick prodigy. However, Fàbregas soon had other things on his mind. Little more than a month after his arrival, Wenger named him in the

first team for a League Cup tie at home to Rotherham United. Arsenal's 'reserve' team prevailed on penalties and he became the club's youngest-ever first team player, aged 16 years and 177 days.

In the next round, in a 5-1 thumping of Wolves at Highbury, Fàbregas scored his first ever goal for Arsenal. It was possibly the easiest chance he would ever have, an open goal tap-from a metre out. Never mind. Wearing the number 57 shirt, he had become the youngest goalscorer in Arsenal's long and illustrious history. He made one more appearance in that 2003-04 season, as a substitute in a victory over West Brom at the Hawthorns in the next round of the League Cup. It was the 'Invincibles' season, so no more first-team opportunities arose, but he had caught the manager's attention.

If fans were shocked to see the young Spaniard sporting a mullet hairstyle at Cardiff for the 2004 Community Shield, few were surprised to see the 17-year-old in the starting line-up. Over the summer

Fàbregas had gained four inches and added a whole lot of muscle; the boy had become a man. He had impressed in pre-season friendlies and with the departure of Ray Parlour and Patrick Vieira injured, he was given his place alongside Gilberto in the midfield.

With three minutes remaining and Arsenal beating Manchester United 3-1, he left the field that day to a standing ovation. In dominating a United midfield, he had announced himself on the grand stage. 'He's only 17, he's better than Roy Keane,' sang the fans all the way home from Cardiff, while *Guardian* writer Kevin McCarra enthused: 'So confident, so sensitive to weight and angle of pass was Cesc Fàbregas that he could have been hailed as an ideal replacement for Vieira until you wrenched your attention from his performance and applied it to his age.'

The following week Fàbregas made his league debut in a 4-1 victory at Everton. At 17 years 103 days he became the club's youngest ever Premier League player. With Vieira still injured, he played four

◀ A young Fàbregas makes his Arsenal debut in a Carling Cup game against Rotherham United in 2003

▼ Sporting a mullet haircut and scoring Arsenal's 5th goal in the Community Shield when the Gunners played Manchester United, 2004

consecutive games in his new number 15 shirt. In the third of them, at Blackburn Rovers, he deflected a Gilberto header to register his first league goal. He is still the club's youngest league scorer.

By now the mullet had disappeared, but the impression he made on staff and fans was set in stone. Despite his size and age, here was a player with the maturity and skill to fit effortlessly into a side who had not been beaten for over 40 games. It was clear to all that Arsène Wenger had unearthed a diamond.

In September 2004, Fàbregas signed his first professional contract and from then on, if not on the bench, he was selected in place of the injured Vieira

▶ Fàbregas celebrates opening the scoring for Arsenal in their Champions League tie with Juventus in 2006

▼ Fàbregas holds off Lucas Neill of Blackburn Rovers at Highbury in 2004

or Gilberto. It was as an unused substitute that he became embroiled in the notorious brawl after Arsenal lost their unbeaten record at Old Trafford. In 2017, on Sky TV's *A Game of Their Own*, he confirmed the long-held suspicion that he was the phantom thrower (frisbee-style according to Martin Keown) of the pizza that hit Alex Ferguson. Reason alone, some Gooners would say, for his status as a club legend!

In his first season, Fàbregas made 33 league appearances and scored twice. He also played in the Champions League and in most games of the FA Cup run. He played 86 minutes of the Cup final victory

against Manchester United, once again coming face to face with Roy Keane and memorably winning a 50-50 challenge that left the United hard man on the ground.

Patrick Vieira left the club in the summer of 2005. Wenger had determined that while either could play with Gilberto Silva, Fàbregas and Vieira together were not a great fit. Such was his belief in the 18-year-old, that he was prepared to let a great player leave the club. In later years Patrick Vieira jokingly introduced Fàbregas as 'the kid who forced me out of Arsenal'.

Instead of imitating the irreplaceable, Fàbregas asserted his own style of play. Of smaller build and less aggressive in his tackling than Vieira, he dominated with his energy, positional sense, and astute and accurate passing.

HE DOMINATED WITH ENERGY, POSITIONAL SENSE AND ACCURATE PASSING

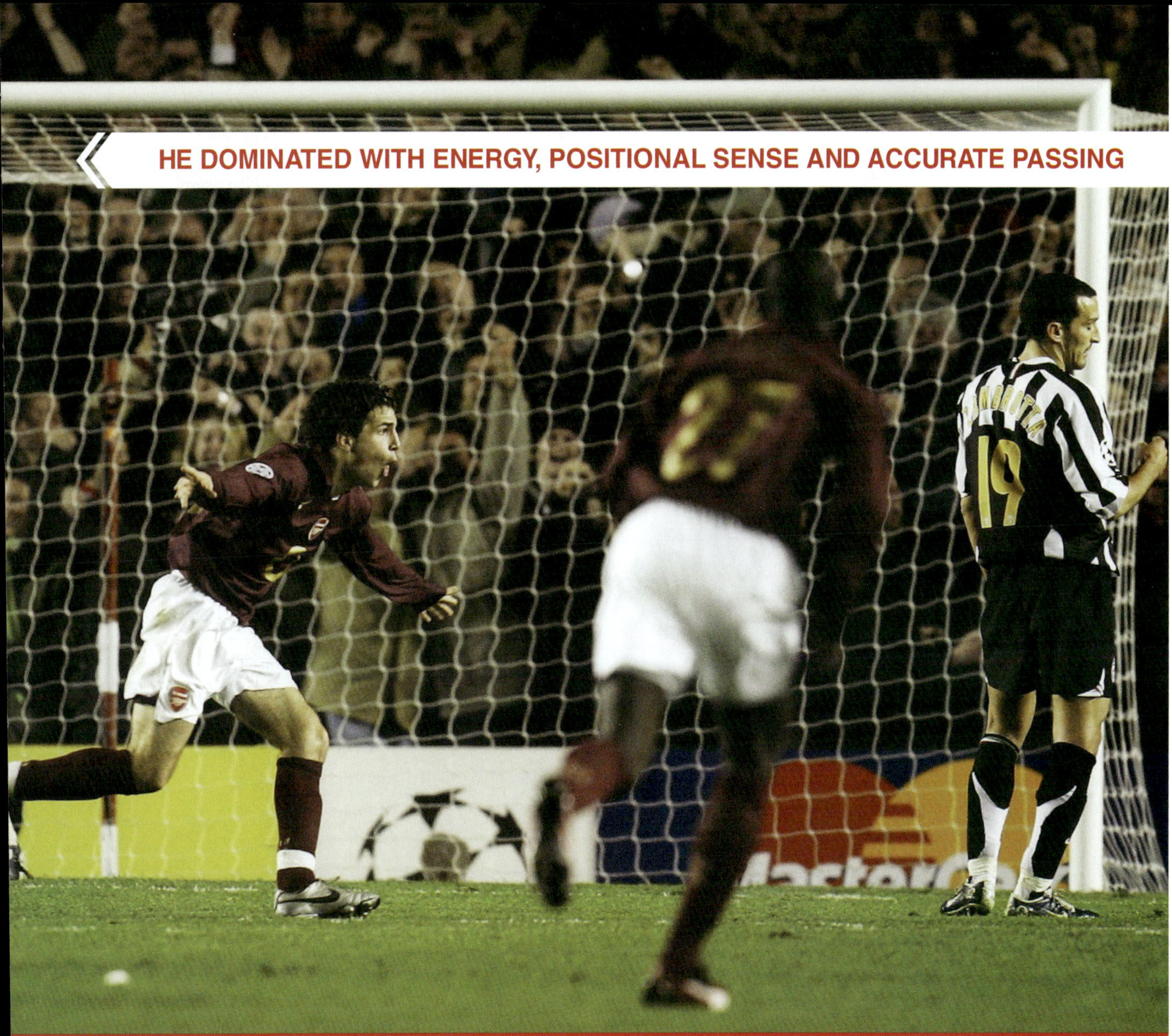

He made 50 appearances in all competitions during the 2005-06 season (more than any other Arsenal player) and amassed 13 assists, the second highest in the league.

Fàbregas also played a major part in the club reaching that season's Champions League final. He scored a brace in an early tie against Dinamo Zagreb and in the round of 16, was instrumental in defeating Real Madrid at the Bernabéu, providing the pass for Thierry Henry's decisive goal. Most memorable was his performance against Vieira, when Juventus visited Highbury in the quarter-finals. He not only dominated the former Gunner in midfield (including one crunching tackle), but scored the opener and set up Henry for the second.

Giving the number 4 shirt to the young star was a clear sign that Wenger intended Cesc to be the lynchpin of his evolving young team. The move to Emirates Stadium had stifled the club's spending ability, just as the double Double-winning team was breaking up, and with the loss of Bergkamp, Pires, Cole and others, so much rested on the teenager's shoulders. His maturity and talent shone through, though, and he played in every league match of the 2006-7 season. He was nominated for both PFA Players' Player of the Year and PFA Young Player of the Year, was named Arsenal's player of the season, and won the Golden Boy award for best young player in Europe.

With Thierry Henry's exit before the 2007-08 season, Fàbregas became the key figure in Arsenal's play. He

▲ Fàbregas remained a star for Arsenal through some patchy times for the Gunners

▶ Scoring for the Gunners when Arsenal played Inter Milan in a Champions League match in 2008

rose to the occasion, consistently proving the creative force of the team. He was at the hub of a side as good as any Wenger had produced. They topped the table until March and reached 60 points earlier than any other team since the introduction of three-point wins. He scored 11 goals in his first 13 games, including vital strikes against Manchester City and United, as well as at Spurs and Liverpool. His superb 30-yard strike goal set the Gunners on the way to becoming the first team to beat AC Milan at the San Siro, but a quarter-final defeat to Liverpool put paid to Fàbregas's chances of a Champions League winner's medal.

In possibly his best year, he was Arsenal's player of the season again and collected the PFA Young Player of the Year award.

Though still only 21, Cesc was named Arsenal captain in November 2008. Wenger also adopted a 4-3-3 formation which gave him a much more attacking role. His positioning was further forward and he had the licence to spearhead the team's counter-attacks. Unfortunately a ligament injury led to him missing nearly four months from the New Year. The following season, the strategy bore fruit as he was the club's leading scorer with 19 goals and made the most assists (15) in 36 appearances.

Fàbregas' final season at the club was 2010-11. Once again, Arsenal were challenging for the title, but his own injury problems contributed to a poor run from February and he also missed the League Cup final defeat. Arguably, his move 'home' to Barcelona, which dragged on for far too long, and subsequent transfer Chelsea, diminished his legacy for some fans. He was also

perhaps unfortunate to be tasked with leading the team in a difficult period, but his record of just one FA Cup in his time at Arsenal is no reflection on his contribution or indeed his captaincy. Between 2006-07 and 2010—11 Fàbregas made more assists than any player in the top leagues of England, Spain, Italy, Germany and France. He was a world-class midfielder, capable of performing a defensive role or creating chances with incisive passing, and he was truly a joy to watch.

▶ Fàbregas seen wearing the captain's armband alongside Rio Ferdinand, as Arsenal prepared to take on Manchester United at Old Trafford

DAVID SEAMAN

RECOGNISED AS ONE OF THE GREATEST KEEPERS OF HIS ERA

Through the 1990s and beyond, 'Safe Hands' was Arsenal's No 1. Among the world's greatest goalkeepers of his era, he played over 500 matches for the club winning three Premier League titles, four FA Cups and one EFL Cup with the Gunners. As England's first choice keeper, he played 75 games in 15 consecutive years.

▶ David Seaman, ready and waiting for goalmouth action

◀ Trading card of Seaman

536 APPEARANCES
0 GOALS

DAVID SEAMAN

69

By the time he arrived in North London, David Seaman was a mature and established goalkeeper. At only 19 years old he had been released by his boyhood club, Leeds United, and then began a decade-long journey to the top. He started at Peterborough United before moving on to Birmingham City, with whom he won promotion to the top flight. Although he was subsequently unable to prevent their immediate relegation, his personal performances earned him a move to Queens Park Rangers. At the West London club, despite keeping goal on a 'plastic' (AstroTurf) pitch, his stock rose even further as he helped them to a League Cup final and fifth place in the (old) First Division. In 1988, his third year at the club, he won his first England cap.

John Lukic had been the Arsenal keeper since the title-winning season of 1988-89. He was very popular with Arsenal fans, but manager George Graham clearly believed Seaman was a better option. When rumours of an imminent signing emerged fans even staged a demonstration. Graham's first attempt to bring the Yorkshireman to Highbury on deadline day in April 1990 failed when Lukic refused to go out to QPR on loan, but in the summer Graham finally got his man. Arsenal paid £1.3 million, which was then a British record for a goalkeeper, while Lukic went back to Leeds, where, in an ironic twist, he had once been a mentor to the teenage Seaman.

At least one familiar face was there to greet Seaman, who was now 27, when he arrived at Highbury. The goalkeeping coach at the time was Arsenal's 1971 Double-winner Bob Wilson, who had also been a coach at QPR for a day a week. Although their styles were rather different, Wilson appreciated how talented Seaman was and in return the new keeper acknowledged the way in which the former Gunner helped him, especially when it came to building his confidence in the lead-up to a game.

On 25 August 1990, as Arsenal travelled to Wimbledon for the opening league game of the season,

ARSENAL LEGENDS

◀ A save from Seaman on his debut for Arsenal against Wimbledon in 1990

▼ Ecstatic FA Cup celebrations, following Arsenal's victory over Sheffield Wednesday in 1993

the name Seaman appeared for the first time in the Gunners' line-up. In front of him was a back four he would get very used to playing with: Dixon, Adams, Bould and Winterburn. Seaman kept a clean sheet that day as Arsenal won 3-0 and impressively he would only concede three in his first five matches. By that point his performances had already converted an initially unconvinced Arsenal faithful.

In fact, Arsenal conceded just 18 goals that season as they regained the title. The new keeper's performances were critical to that miserly defence. Among his notable performances, he rescued a point at White Hart Lane with a save which bewildered his England co-star Gary Lineker; he made a series of world-class saves in a cup tie against Leeds; and thwarted Liverpool; and John Barnes in particular, in the crucial 1-0 win at Anfield. He also came second in ITV's 'Saves of the Season' with his stunning full-length fingertip save to deny Sunderland's Gary Owers at Roker Park. The only blot on a remarkably consistent season was being beaten by Paul Gascoigne's 35-metre free-kick in the FA Cup semi-final at Wembley, as Spurs ended Arsenal's bid for the Double.

As George Graham's team slowly ran out of steam, Arsenal became cup-hunters rather than title-hunters, with Seaman's efforts often to thank for their success. In their run to the 1993 FA Cup final his incredible low save from a Lee Chapman header helped them overcome Leeds United, while back at Wembley for the semi-final he was integral to Arsenal withstanding great pressure as they avenged the previous defeat to Spurs.

DAVID SEAMAN

Chris Waddle's shot for Sheffield Wednesday beat him in the replay of the final to force extra time, although fortunately Andy Linighan scored in the last minute (famously with two broken fingers and a broken nose) to deliver FA Cup victory for the Gunners.

Seaman also had a major role in Arsenal's 1994 Cup-Winners' Cup triumph when, having played a blinder to keep out Paris Saint-Germain in the semi-final, he repeated the feat in the final against Parma in Copenhagen, where he was only able to play after

receiving pain-killing-injections and wearing a special cast to protect his injured rib. Nevertheless, he was the mainstay of a classic rearguard action. He prevented a Gianfranco Zola strike with a great tip over the bar, pulled off a world-class stop from Faustino Asprilla and denied Zola again in the final minutes.

By 1994-95, George Graham's last season at the club, Seaman was at last being recognised as one of the best keepers in the country. Even England manager Graham Taylor, who had often overlooked him, made him his number one choice. As Arsenal continued to be a cup team, a new facet of Seaman's goalkeeping had emerged: he was a penalty-saving specialist. In a League Cup tie he saved three of Millwall's four efforts in the shoot-out, while in the semi-final of the 1995 Cup-Winners' Cup, he saved another three to progress past Sampdoria to the final. For all his heroics, most

▲ Pulling off a crucial catch for the Gunners when they faced AJ Auxerre in the Cup-Winners' Cup quarter-final second leg, 1995

◄ David Seaman and Lee Dixon share a joke

DAVID SEAMAN

73

still remember him backpedalling in vain to prevent Nayim's shot from the half-way line in Arsenal's defeat in the final. Such is the goalkeeper's lot.

Arsène Wenger's arrival signalled a new era for the club, but in the team's back five life remained very much the same. However, although he rarely missed games through injury, David was forced to miss the first half of the 1996-97 season after a freak accident where he damaged his knee ligaments bending down to pick up a TV remote. His return marked an upturn in Arsenal's form under the new manager and they never looked back. He was a central figure in the 1997-98 Double-winning campaign and in the following season played in all 38 Premier League games, conceding just 17 goals.

In 1996, David Seaman was nominated for the Ballon d'Or and was recognised as one of the 20 best players in the world. Through to his second Double winning season in 2001-02, he remained among the best goalkeepers on the planet. He was renowned for his desire to improve, and trained hard and long. His keeping was not flamboyant, but calm, strong and consistent. He had a presence in front of goal possessed by only the great. His positioning was both strategic — he kept a high line despite rare but high-profile incidents — and instinctive — his shot-stopping displayed a magnificent agility for such a big man — and his distribution became an integral feature of Arsenal's counter-attacking tactics.

David Seaman was a Yorkshireman, but belied the stereotype with a constant smile and an often-heard hearty chuckle. He also developed his own look with a career-spanning hefty moustache, long sideburns and shiny, full-bodied hair tied up in a ponytail. Everything about him, down to his self-adopted nickname, 'Safe Hands', emanated confidence. Only after the 2002 World Cup, when he was caught off his line by Ronaldinho's long-range free-kick did his powers seem to be waning. He was now in his late 30s, but remained England's number one for another two years.

The 2002-03 season was to be Seaman's last at the club, although he still managed 43 games in the campaign, including most of the journey to the FA Cup final. The semi-final against Sheffield United at Old Trafford in 2003 was his 1,000th senior appearance and he marked the occasion with something special. With six minutes left and Arsenal hanging on to a 1-0 lead, a miss-hit shot lobbed up for an unmarked Paul Peschisolido, two metres from goal. His flicked header was a certain goal, but David had other ideas. Arching his spine as he dived backwards, he stretched his arm and reached to claw the ball off the line. It is still regarded as one of the great saves in English football and many extend that to the world.

The subsequent FA Cup Final was his final match for the Gunners. Made captain for the day, his focus was as sharp as ever, proven by a great save from Brett Ormerod's rocket of a volley from a tight angle. Lifting the cup — his ninth major trophy with the club — in front of ecstatic fans was a most fitting end to a fabulous Arsenal career.

After 13 years of service, David Seaman left the club on a free transfer to Manchester City, choosing to continue playing rather than take the coaching role offered at Highbury. He played against Arsenal in a defeat at Maine Road, but had retired from football before the fans were able to show their appreciation in the return fixture at Highbury later in the season. He has returned to the club since as an occasional goalkeeping coach at the Academy and every time he visits the Emirates he receives the warm appreciation he deserves as a great player and magnificent servant of the club.

▼ Seaman makes a spectacular save from Paul Peschisolido to deny Sheffield Wednesday a goal in their FA Cup semi-final clash in 2003

FREDDIE LJUNGBERG

LJUNGBERG

HE PROVIDED ENERGY, FLAMBOYANCY AND COMPOSURE

He was the flame-haired super-Swede who provided energy and bustling play to match the flamboyant style of the 'Invincibles'. But there was more to Freddie Ljungberg than good looks and incessant running. He was a master at finding space in the area, unruffled in possession and the most composed of finishers.

▶ Freddie Ljungberg — super-Swede

◀ Ljungberg had presence on and off the field of play

328 APPEARANCES
72 GOALS

FREDDIE LJUNGBERG

The word was already out on the teenager who had helped Halmstads to become Swedish champions in 1997. Playing for the first team since he was 17 years old, he was clearly destined for stardom. While the big guns of Europe, including Arsenal, had sent their scouts to watch the energetic midfielder, all Arsène Wenger needed was to watch him on TV. Ljungberg ran

England's defenders ragged all night as Glenn Hoddle's men suffered defeat in Stockholm in 1998. With rumours of Chelsea being close to securing Ljungberg's signature, the Arsenal boss moved quickly, pushing through the £3 million deal to bring the now 20-year-old to Highbury.

Ljungberg's Arsenal debut came against Manchester United at Highbury. The Gunners were cruising with a

◀ With his distinctive flame red striped hair, Ljungberg challenges for the ball when Arsenal played Juventus in the Champions League, 2001

Partly through hip and ankle injuries and partly through Wenger managing Ljungberg's adjustment to English football, he only made 14 starts that season. He came on as a substitute in the drawn FA Cup semi-final against Manchester United and might have been the hero if his late shot had evaded Schmeichel. He then started in the replay, when Arsenal was defeated in the famous 'greatest semi-final ever'. In both those matches, Ljungberg had replaced Marc Overmars on the right wing, having always played as a number 10 or in central midfield. It was a steep learning curve for a young player in a new country, but it was clear that Wenger believed he was just as capable of influencing the game from a wide position.

In the summer of 1999, Arsenal signed Thierry Henry from Juventus. They were a similar age, had both come from abroad and they soon became close friends. They also quickly learned to complement each other's play on the field: the Swede's energy, work-rate and passing ability was a perfect match for the French striker's flair and eye for goal. Ljungberg proved a fast learner and rapidly became a first team regular. In 1999-2000 he made 43 appearances across all competitions, although he missed the 2000 UEFA Cup final due to a rib injury.

2-0 lead, so Wenger gave the new Swede a 12-minute acclimatising cameo at the end of the match. He had been on the pitch just six minutes when he nipped onto a mis-hit Stephen Hughes pass and casually lobbed it over Schmeichel. The fans immediately fell in love with their new fresh-faced, grinning youngster and would cherish him for years to come.

By then, he was commonly known to fans as Freddie (a nickname he never had in Sweden) after early Gooner attempts to call him, 'Kid Vicious' due to his Mohican-esque hairstyle, failed to catch on. They loved his commitment, his boundless running and his motivating, pumping clenched fists. When he added a scarlet streak to his hair a new song emerged

and echoed around Highbury: 'We love you Freddie, because you've got red hair, we love you Freddie, because you're everywhere.'

In the 2000-01 season, fans began to realise just how good Freddie — still only 23 years old — could be. He was an intelligent player, quickly building up an understanding with his teammates, while his runs from deep were developing into yet another weapon for a team already brimming with attacking options. He scored nine goals over the season and the one that gave Arsenal the lead in the 2001 FA Cup final was a perfect example of how he could run into space in dangerous areas. Picked out by Robert Pires' pass, his finish was cool and deadly accurate.

The disappointment of finishing as runners-up in league and cup drove Ljungberg — and the team — to an even higher standard in the following season. He now seemed to have a telepathic relationship with Robert Pires and Dennis Bergkamp, who fed his rapier runs into the box. His finishing eschewed flashiness for a calm and decisive strike. And he had become the man for the big occasion. He brought Arsenal back into the game in

▲ Scoring for the Gunners in the 2001 FA Cup final

▶ Ljungberg cradles both the FA Cup and the Premiership trophies in Arsenal's double winning year, 2001-02

and sublime skill as he dribbled from his own half and executed a sumptuous curling shot to double Arsenal's lead over Chelsea. He was given the man of the match award and ended the season with 17 goals. He was named Arsenal's player of the season and received the Barclaycard player of the year award.

An operation on a cartilage tear on his hip incurred during World Cup duty with Sweden kept him out of the first ten games of the 2002-03 season. In his first game back, he finished a wonderful sweeping team move to help see off Borussia Dortmund in the Champions League. He suffered another injury — this time his ankle — late in the season, returning to hit a hat-trick in a 4-1 win at Sunderland in the final league match. A few days later, Arsenal's FA Cup talisman was back at Wembley for a third successive final. Ljungberg

a crucial win over Manchester United, scored the winner for the 10-man Gunners at Anfield and got a brace in the famous victory over Juventus, the second of which he began in his own half and ended with a brave finish after a magical pass from Bergkamp.

When Pires, who had been in scintillating form, was injured at the beginning of the run-in to the end of that season it was Ljungberg who stepped up. He scored in five successive matches, helping the Gunners put on a title-winning run. He then secured Arsenal's FA Cup final triumph, showing pace, strength

FREDDIE LJUNGBERG

converted when Sylvain Wiltord's shot came off the post to score the only goal of the semi-final against Sheffield United. In the final, it was his touch that set up Pires' goal and the win.

Ljungberg had done enough by then to secure his place in Arsenal history. He was established as not just a brilliant player, but also a style icon. His high cheekbones, chiselled jawline and now shaved head ('We love you Freddie, because you've got no hair') made him prime Highbury eye-candy, while his love of clothes put him alongside David Beckham as a high-fashion footballer. In 2004, as billboards and ads of him in just his Calvin Klein underwear were everywhere, while *Sun* readers voted him sexiest player in the Premier League.

When fit, Ljungberg was virtually guaranteed a spot in Wenger's team. He could play on either wing or centrally; just behind the striker where his instinctive and perfectly

timed darts into the area paid massive dividends. He could also be relied upon to get back and defend. When the team needed to battle he was in the thick of it. In an era when Arsenal's disciplinary record was under scrutiny, Ljungberg (after a single dismissal at Tottenham in his first season) received just the occasional yellow card.

He was an integral member of the 'Invincibles' team, playing 30 matches in the unbeaten season. He scored four league goals and once again the FA Cup brought something special from the super-Swede. He hit two goals (one after a quality pull-back and the other a rare header) playing as a makeshift striker against Middlesbrough in the fourth round and another brace in the 5-1 demolition of Portsmouth in the quarter-final. Unfortunately, though, he was unable to help them overcome Manchester United to make a fourth successive final.

Ljungberg's play continued to be an important facet of the free-flowing Arsenal team. His boundless running

and no-frills passing in counter attacks were equal to his close control in a crowded box, late bursts into the area and ability to pounce on a loose ball. He appeared in his last FA Cup final in 2005 against Manchester United as a 67th-minute substitute replacing Bergkamp. He made two decisive actions; first miraculously deflecting a Van Nistelrooy header off the line and up on to the bar and then coolly slotting home Arsenal's second kick in the penalty shoot-out to help collect his third winner's medal.

He would play another two seasons for the Gunners and remained popular in a transitional team. Always prone to injuries, they now became a threat to his game, especially persistent ankle and hip problems. He also suffered with migraines and even blood poisoning from one of his tattoos. After missing a number of games, he returned for the 2006 Champions League quarter-final second leg against Real Madrid,

both semi-finals with Villarreal and played in the final in Paris, a match he describes as his biggest disappointment in football.

When Ljungberg limped off during a game at Tottenham Hotspur on 21 April 2007, it proved to be his last game for Arsenal. He returned to the club as a youth coach in 2016 and then as an under-23 coach in 2018. When Unai Emery was dismissed in 2019 he took over as interim first-team coach for six games before becoming Mikael Arteta's assistant until August 2020. He remains one of the most popular players to have worn the red and white in the 21st century.

▲ Controlling the ball for Arsenal when they played Barcelona in the Champions League final, 2006

◄ Freddie modelling for Calvin Klein

SAKA
BUKAYO SAKA

PACEY, CONTROLLED SHARPNESS IN FRONT OF GOAL

Bukayo Saka's pace and control leaves defenders in his wake, his sharpness in front of goal is deadly, and his work rate makes him a special team player. One of the best forwards in world football today, he could yet be the greatest player ever seen in the red and white — and he is one of our own!

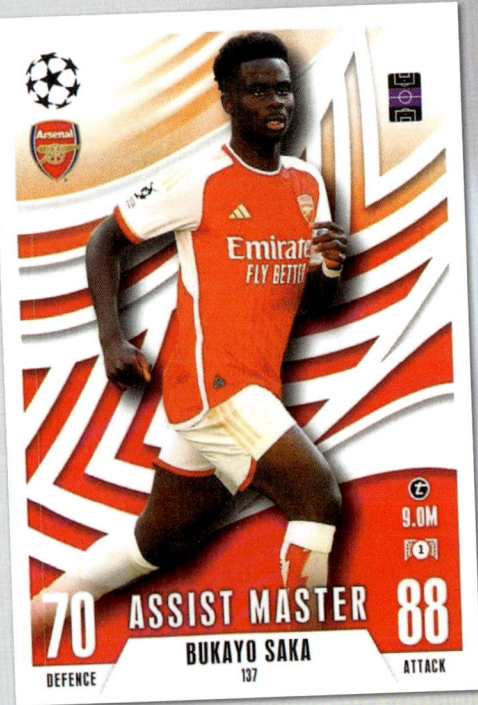

ARSENAL LEGENDS

▶ Arsenal great — Bukayo Saka

◀ Saka trading card

84

195 APPEARANCES
53 GOALS

BUKAYO SAKA

Still in his early 20s, Bukayo Saka has spent almost the entirety of his footballing life at Arsenal. Born in Ealing in West London, he was briefly at Watford, but joined the Gunners' Hale End academy at the age of eight. Liam Brady, then Head of Youth Development, and his team soon realised what a gem they had in the young kid. By the time he was 11 he was the star of his age group and began playing in older teams. At 16 he signed his scholarship contract with the club and was training with the first team. All his academy coaches said the same thing… Here was a model player: talented, bright (As and A*s in his GCSEs), humble, cheerful and eager to learn. He had the world at his feet.

By the time Unai Emery took over as manager, Saka was a valued young member of the squad. In

▶ Saka makes his first team debut for the Gunners in a UEFA Europa League game with Vorskla Poltava in 2018

▼ Bukayo Saka in an Academy match for Arsenal U15 vs Swindon Town in 2016

November 2018, in the penultimate group stage match of the Europa League, he travelled to Kiev to face Vorskla Poltava in temperatures of -14°C, replacing Aaron Ramsey in the 68th minute, and making his Arsenal debut at the age of 17 years and 86 days. Emery would give the young star a couple of chances as the 2018-19 season progressed, including a seven-minute Premier League debut (the first player born

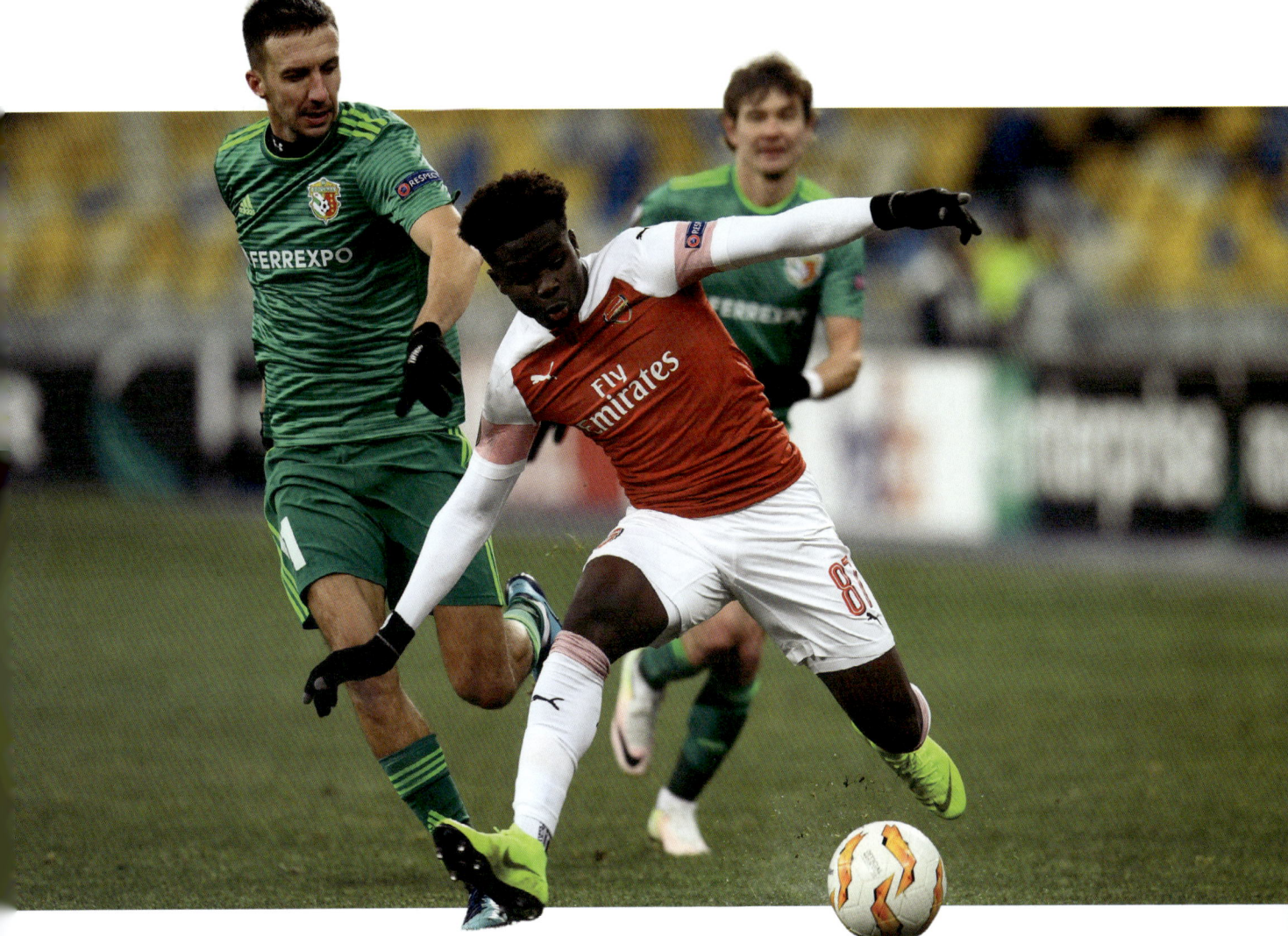

in 2001 to play in a Premier League match) in a 4-0 defeat of Everton. He was an unused substitute at Baku for the Europa League final and received a runners-up medal after the defeat to Chelsea.

The Europa League proved Saka's springboard in the following season. Wearing the number 77 shirt, he starred as a left-sided forward in a 3-0 win away at Eintracht Frankfurt in the first match of the campaign. He made two and scored his first goal for Arsenal, an emphatic curling strike from the edge of the area. Just as he established himself under Emery, the manager was replaced by Mikel Arteta. With his assistant, Freddie Ljungberg, having helped coach Saka since he was 15, Arteta kept faith and even played him at left-back when injuries forced his hand.

However, despite playing many games in his unflavoured position, Saka was not to be denied his breakthrough season. The 18-year-old played 38

times across all four competitions. As the season drew to a close, he netted his first Premier League goal, hooking a loose ball home in a 2-0 win over Wolves. Once again, though, he was an unused Cup final substitute, but this time picked up a winner's medal after the victory against Chelsea and was voted third in Arsenal's player of the season poll.

Despite quite often being required to fill in at left-back, Saka's 12 assists in the 2019-20 season were more than any other Arsenal player and his tricky wing work was becoming a great source of chances for the Gunners. With close control and penetrating dribbles he could weave his way past multiple defenders. His pace scared those assigned to mark him, and his crosses and ability to spot a killer pass were improving season by season: his outrageous nutmeg of a Newcastle United defender to set up Nicolas Pépé for a simple tap-in was particularly savoured by fans.

BUKAYO SAKA

Saka was proving a tough customer, too. Often given rough treatment by opposing defenders he was able to withstand the kicks and get back to his feet. Considering that he has been in the top ten most fouled players in every season he's played, until 2025 he only missed a single game in most campaigns and a handful in two others.

In July 2020 Saka's new long-term contract demonstrated how much he had progressed, and the faith Arteta and the club had in their winger. He was given the vacant number seven shirt, following in the footsteps of many Arsenal greats, including Liam Brady and Robert Pires. The manager said of his young charge, 'He represents every value that this football club stands for.' The 2020-21 season was to be a difficult one for the Gunners as they often struggled defensively, but Saka was a bright light. Once again, he stepped up a level and his performances earned him a regular place in the team as a forward. Increasingly, he was venturing infield from a wide position, marauding through the space in the central areas of the pitch or creating chances as he ran across the opposition's holding defensive line.

▲ Saka wearing the number 77 shirt for Arsenal in 2020. Sticking with a similar theme, he was later upgraded to the coveted number seven for his efforts in the team

▲ Celebrating scoring for Arsenal when they played Wolves in an empty stadium in 2020, due to the Covid-19 pandemic

Saka's first goal of the season came with a rare headed effort against Sheffield United and he was called up to make his debut for the senior England team in a 3-0 win over Wales in October 2020. However, it was Boxing Day 2021 when many fans realised his true potential. In a man-of-the-match performance capped by a long-range lob over Édouard Mendy, he inspired Arsenal to a 3-1 defeat of Chelsea that ended a miserable run of seven games without a win. He then scored or made assists in all but one of their next five unbeaten matches.

At the end of the 2020-21 season, Saka had become the second youngest player (after Cesc Fàbregas) to make 50 appearances for the Gunners. He finished the season once again as the club's leading assist-maker with seven and notched the same amount of goals. He won three consecutive Arsenal player of the month awards between December and February and was voted player of the season.

At Euro 2020 (held in 2021 due to Covid), Saka, still only 18 years old, became England's youngest ever player in a major tournament. He had a major role in their journey to the final as both a winger and a wing-back. However, it was a bittersweet experience as he, along with Marcus Rashford and Jadon Sancho, suffered disgusting racist abuse after missing in the penalty shoot-out in the final. It is testament to his

BUKAYO SAKA

character that Saka went on, yet again, to have his best season in his career.

He was the club's leading scorer in 2021-22 with 14 goals, the pick of them coming against Spurs at the Emirates, when he wove his way past two defenders in the area to score, and a coolly directed first-time strike against champions Manchester City. He made another seven assists and for a consecutive season was Arsenal's player of the season. He was also nominated for the Premier League player of the season, Premier League young player of the season and PFA young player of the year.

By the beginning of 2023, Bukayo Saka had become an Arsenal icon and placed in or near the top ten players in the world in many lists. He had grown as a personality and a player. He added an ability to find pockets of space, characteristic stop-start runs, and presented a constant threat to cut inside and deliver a curling shot. He was also now established as the team's penalty-taker, two years on from the Euros shoot-out miss. Now with 100 Premier League games under his belt, he scored 15 times in the 2022-23 season — a selection of cool finishes, shots from the tightest of angles and screamers, such as the one that helped defeat Manchester United at the Emirates. He won the PFA young player of the year award and was England men's player of the year.

Saka had broken into the team at a low point in the

◀ Saka scores for the Gunners when they met Real Madrid in the Champions League semi-final in 2025

▶ Showing poise and perfect ball control

club's fortunes and was key to their transformation into Premier League challengers. Across all competitions in the 2023-24 season he increased his goal contributions yet again, with 20 goals and 14 assists. He also set a club record with his 83rd consecutive Premier League appearance for Arsenal, captained the team for the first time, played his 200th match for the Gunners, amassed a half-century of goals and, at Euro 2024, became Arsenal's all-time leading scorer for the England national team.

However, 2024-25 proved to be a deeply frustrating season for the now 23-year-old forward. His form was scintillating in the early months as he became the youngest Arsenal player to net 50 Premier League goals, but a hamstring injury, his first major injury in senior football, kept him out for the first quarter of 2025 and hampered the team's title chase. On his return, as a substitute against Fulham, he scored with a stooping back post header and then became the fourth-youngest player to reach 100 goals and assists in the Premier League. He helped Arsenal seal a place in the Champions League semi-final with a delicious chipped finish over Real Madrid's keeper Thibaut Courtois and then netted in the semi-final, too, as Arsenal fought in vain to overcome PSG.

Bukayo Saka is already a true Arsenal legend. His thrilling style, assists, goals and personality have all been a major influence in shaping the identity of today's club. All that is missing is for him to play in a trophy-winning side. He has come tantalisingly close to fulfilling this ambition, and no doubt all fans fervently hope that he will achieve it in the near future with the club that he loves and that adores him.

TOP 50 GREATEST PLAYERS OF ALL TIME

It goes without saying that to make it on to this list you must have been — or in some cases still are — special. You must have had talent, vision and the determination to win. All the players featured here, and there are some big names as well as a few that won't be quite so familiar, possessed those qualities, but above that what they all had in common is that they wore the red and white shirt with immense pride.

▶ A team full of legends — Arsenal

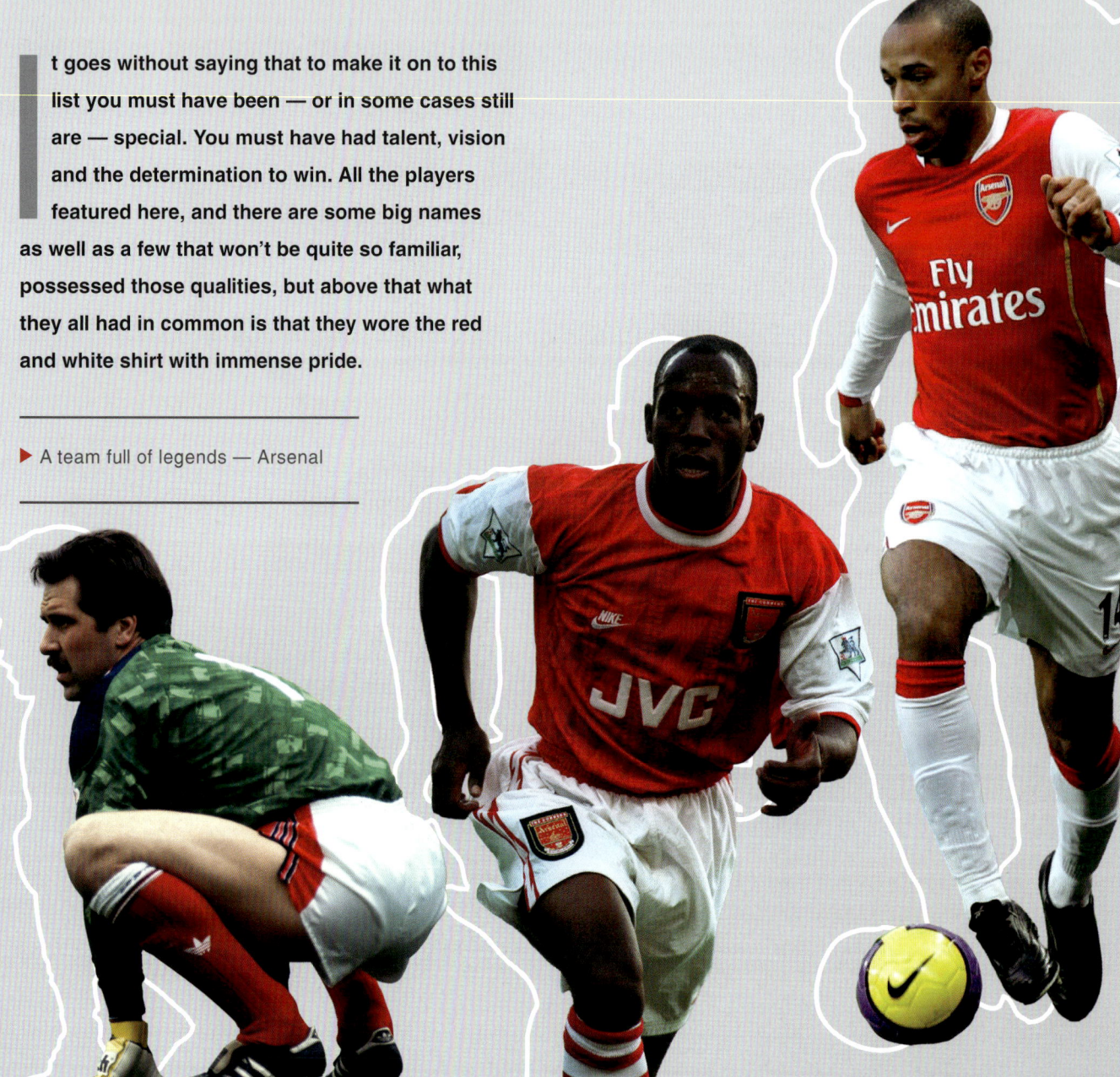

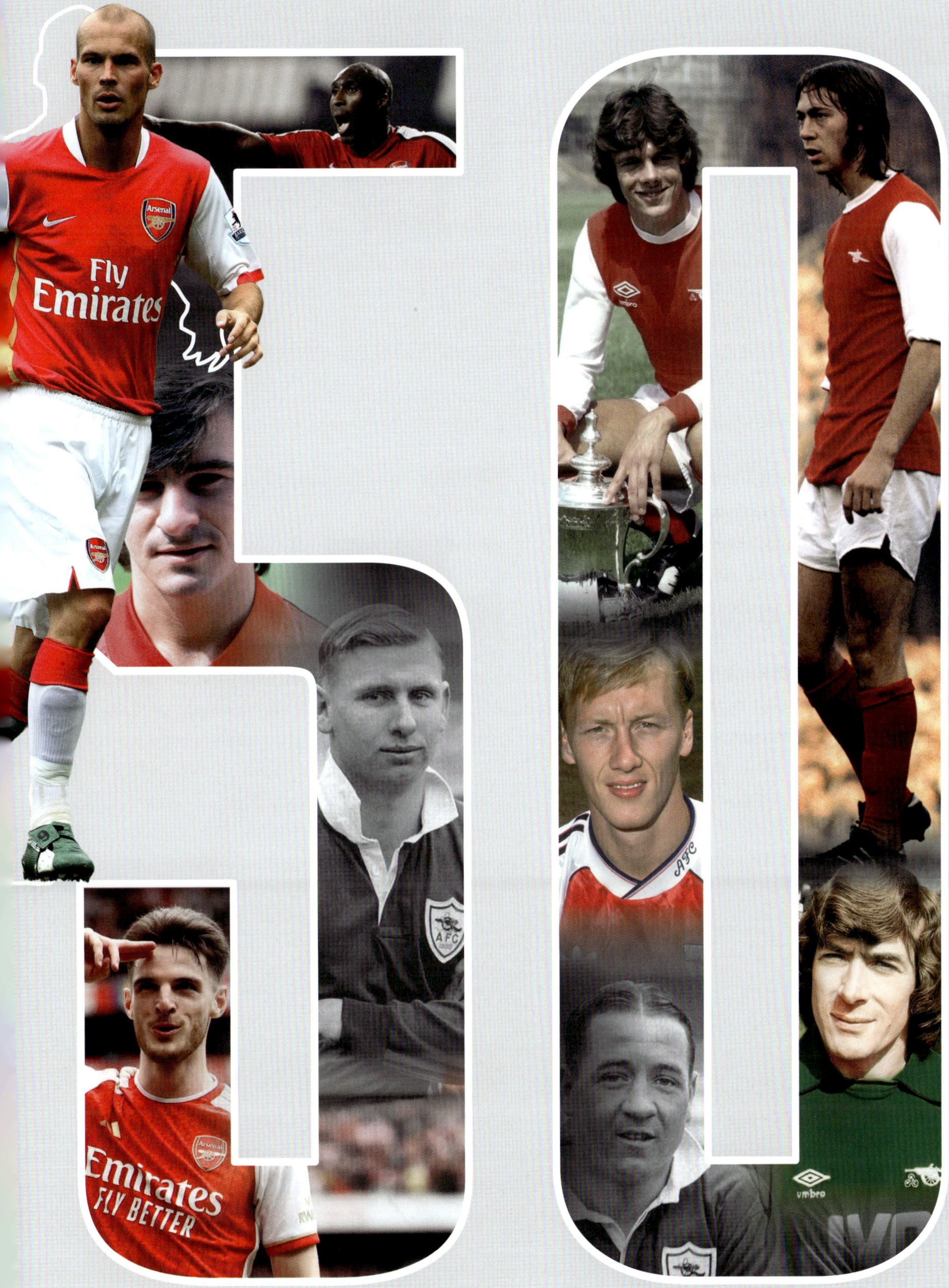
Fly
Emirates
Emirates
FLY BETTER

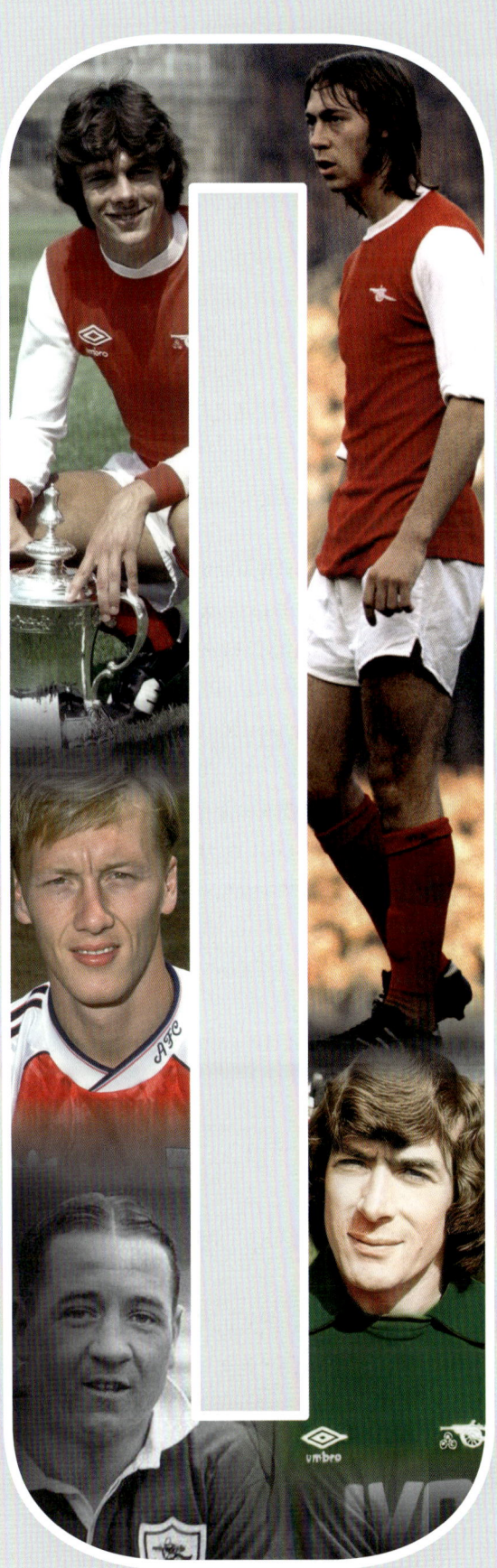

50 NICOLAS ANELKA

Still 17 when he arrived in early 1997, an Ian Wright injury meant Frenchman Anelka quickly broke into the first team and was a vital element in the 1997-98 Premier League and FA Cup Double, scoring in the Cup final against Newcastle. The following season he was top scorer and PFA Young Player of the Year, but it wasn't a successful campaign for Arsenal. Fans suggested Anelka wasn't trying and, after 90 appearances and 28 goals, he moved to Real Madrid in August 1999. Often a controversial figure, Anelka was nonetheless a talented striker who made his mark and later admitted he probably shouldn't have left North London when he did.

49 ASHLEY COLE

In 2000, 18-year-old Ashley Cole signed for the club he supported as a boy, establishing himself as first-choice left-back in 2000-01. Always an attacking player, he won the Premier title in 2002 and 2004, and the FA Cup in 2002, 2003 and 2005. However, in 2005 he was 'tapped up' by Chelsea, subsequently receiving a hefty fine for secretly discussing a move, and this soured his relationship with the club and fans. He was injured for most of 2005-06, but played in the 2006 Champions League final against Barcelona, which Arsenal lost. He then completed that move to Chelsea, having scored nine goals in 228 appearances for Arsenal.

48 MICHAEL THOMAS

A versatile player, strong in the tackle and dynamic with the ball, Thomas played at full-back, centre-back and

midfield in his career. It was as an assured box-to-box midfielder that he established himself in George Graham's team. He won a League Cup medal with the Gunners as a substitute in the 1987 final and wrote his name in the Arsenal history books for his added-time goal in the league title decider at Anfield in 1989. The London-born, Spurs-supporting midfielder made 206 appearances and scored 30 goals for the Gunners before moving to Liverpool in 1991, where he scored in their 1992 FA Cup final triumph.

47 FRANK STAPLETON

Born in Dublin and later a Republic of Ireland stalwart, Frank Stapleton was a powerful centre-forward who was particularly strong in the air. He made his first-team debut in 1975 and spent eight years at the club. Notably, he played in three consecutive Cup finals, getting the second goal in 1979's famous 'five-minute final' victory over Manchester United (so called because in the last five minutes United scored twice to equalise, only for Arsenal's Alan Sunderland to get the 89th-minute winner). Stapleton subsequently moved to United, where he won the FA Cup again, twice, and was the first player to get Cup final goals for two different clubs.

46 MESUT ÖZIL

Midfielder Mesut Özil came to Arsenal in 2013, reputedly costing the Gunners £42.5 million, which made him, at the time, the most expensive German player ever. Arsenal hadn't won a trophy in nine years, but Özil was part of the team that broke the curse, beating Hull 3-2 to lift the 2014 FA Cup. The following year they retained it, 4-0 against

Aston Villa, and in 2017 they won it again, beating Chelsea 2-1. Technically skilled, but above all an incredible creative playmaker, Özil wasn't quite the same player after Wenger retired. He left in 2021 on a free transfer to Fenerbahçe with 254 appearances, 44 goals and an impressive 79 assists to his name.

45 ▶ SOL CAMPBELL

Spurs supporters have never forgiven Sol Campbell for switching sides and that bitterness tends to overshadow his qualities as a player for both sets of fans. However, he was an extremely reliable and solid centre-back for the Gunners. First partnered with Tony Adams, who retired after Campbell's first season at the club, then Martin Keown and, latterly, in the Invincibles team, Kolo Touré, forwards simply found him very hard to get past. Between 2001 and 2006 he won a raft of honours with Arsenal, including the Double in that first season, making 197 appearances and scoring 11 goals.

44 ▶ MARTIN KEOWN

Martin Keown spent a season at Arsenal in the mid-1980s, reputedly moving to Aston Villa because manager George Graham refused to pay him £50 extra a week. He went back to Highbury in 1993, under Graham again and then Wenger, and stayed until 2004. Although he was a centre-back, he also played at right-back and left-back, and was a mainstay of a defence that included Tony Adams and Steve Bould. Keown was often

described as combative and he certainly wasn't afraid to get stuck in, but that was very much to Arsenal's advantage. He won three league titles, three FA Cups and a European Cup Winners' Cup.

43 ▶ GABRIEL MARTINELLI

The talented Brazilian signed for Arsenal in the summer of 2019, when he was just 18, but swiftly broke into the first team. Agile, energetic and dynamic, Martinelli was originally a central attacking player, but Arteta has developed him as a winger, who can take the ball past opponents and find pockets of space down the left, to create chances for his teammates or sometimes score himself. Over six seasons with the club perhaps he hasn't been prolific, but his 50-goal tally in all competitions understates the impact he has on the field and he is an enormous asset to the club.

42 ▶ JACK KELSEY

One of the leading lights of Arsenal in the 1950s, Jack Kelsey's first game was in early 1951, in a 5-1 loss to Charlton Athletic — not a great result for a goalie and it took him a couple of seasons to become first-choice keeper. However, he appeared 29 times for the 1952-53 First Division-winning team and was a regular for the next eight years. He was also the Welsh national goalkeeper and played in the 1958 World Cup (Wales' only World Cup finals until 2022), but in 1962 he picked up a back injury in a friendly against Brazil and retired a year later, having played 352 times for Arsenal.

41 ▷ DAVID JACK

At 29, some thought David Jack was too old when Herbert Chapman bought him in 1928 for what was then the eye-watering sum of £10,890. However, in his first season he scored 25 in 31 games and he was a stalwart of the successful 1930s team, first under Chapman and then under George Allison. Playing up front beside players such as Cliff Bastin and Jack Lambert, Jack was part of the 1930 FA Cup-winning side and in 1930-31, as Arsenal won their first ever league title, he scored 34 goals, his highest total. They took the league title again in 1932-33 and 1933-34, the season Jack retired with 124 goals in 208 appearances.

40 ▷ PER MERTESACKER

At 6 foot 6, German centre-back Per Mertesacker stood tall in Arsenal's defence for seven seasons from 2011 to 2018. However, as well as being a formidable presence and powerful in the air, he was also a skilful tackler, who read the game well and was seldom booked. He arrived at Highbury from Werder Bremen and slotted into the side quickly, forming easy partnerships with, first, Frenchman Laurent Koscielny and, then, Belgian Thomas Vermaelen. In particular, he was instrumental in the FA Cup-winning runs of 2013-14 and 2014-15. His last couple of seasons were affected by injury, but Mertesacker has continued his connection with the club and currently manages the Arsenal Academy.

39 ▷ AARON RAMSEY

A three-time FA Cup winner with Arsenal, Aaron Ramsey scored the clincher against Hull City in 2014 and against Chelsea in 2017, as well as playing in the 2015 final against Aston Villa, which Arsenal also won. Born in Wales (and set to become a key Welsh international), Ramsey signed for Arsenal from Cardiff City in 2008. He made his debut for the Gunners at the age of 17, but in 2010 he broke his leg in a Stoke game, which temporarily derailed his career. However, after short spells on loan to Nottingham Forest and Cardiff he regained his fitness and his place in the team, remaining a midfield stalwart until 2019 when he moved to Juventus.

38 ▷ GEORGE ARMSTRONG

A traditional winger, known for his playmaking and imaginative crosses, George Armstrong — always called 'Geordie' at Highbury — arrived at the club in 1962 straight from school. Creative but consistent, he played every game of the Double-winning season — it's often said that he was involved in over half of the goals scored in 1970-71 — and when he departed in 1977 he had made 621 appearances in a red and white shirt, even now a total only exceeded by David O'Leary and Tony Adams. In 1990 he returned to the club as part of George Graham's coaching staff, but died suddenly at the age of 56 in 2000.

37 ▷ CHARLIE NICHOLAS

Nicknamed 'Champagne Charlie' because of his flamboyant lifestyle, Charlie Nicholas was a great but often inconsistent talent, although he could rise to an occasion. Terry Neill signed him from Celtic in 1983, but with Arsenal slipping

down the table Neill was sacked just before Christmas. However, on Boxing Day 1984 Nicholas got two in a 4-2 win over Spurs, making him a fan favourite. Under Don Howe Arsenal's form improved and Nicholas won the 1984 Arsenal Player of the Year. When George Graham became manager in 1986, Nicholas was no longer guaranteed to play, but, crucially, he got both goals against Liverpool in the 1987 League Cup final. In 1988 he left for Aberdeen, having scored 54 goals in 184 Arsenal appearances.

36 ▸ NWANKWO KANU

Nigerian Nwankwo Kanu picked up two FA Cup medals and two Premier League titles during his time with Arsenal, scoring 44 goals in 197 games across all competitions between 1999 and 2004. Thierry Henry was first-choice striker, but Kanu frequently came off the bench to great effect. Unpredictable in attack, in the 1999-2000 season he famously scored a hat-trick in 15 minutes against Chelsea. Arsenal had been losing 2-0, but won 3-2. At the end of the Invincibles era, he moved to West Bromwich Albion, who had just been promoted, and then Portsmouth. He also made 86 appearances for the Nigerian national side.

35 ▸ GEORGE GRAHAM

Although perhaps best known as Arsenal manager, George Graham also had a successful career as a player and about 50% of the games he played were for the Gunners. Having previously turned out for Chelsea and Aston Villa, he first arrived at Highbury in 1966 and was top scorer in 1966-67 and 1967-68, although he subsequently moved to midfield. Nicknamed Stroller for his laid-back style of play, he won the 1970 Inter-Cities Fairs Cup with the club

and was an important part of the 1970-71 Double-winning side, but after 77 goals and 308 appearances he left in 1972 for Manchester United.

34 ▸ ALEX JAMES

A central figure in Arsenal's dominant 1930s side, Scotsman Alex James played as an inside-forward and set the club up for its first major trophy by scoring the opening goal against Huddersfield Town in the 1930 FA Cup final. Arsenal, of course, won 2-0. Not that James was a prolific goalscorer. Rather, he was king of the assists, feeding Cliff Bastin, Ted Drake and David Jack with his pinpoint-accurate passing. League titles in 1930-31, 1932-33, 1933-34 and 1934-35 followed, as did the 1936 FA Cup, with James as captain in a 1-0 victory over Sheffield United. However, age and injury took their toll and he retired in 1937.

33 ▸ ALEXIS SÁNCHEZ

When he arrived at Arsenal Chilean international Alexis Sánchez was already a big name and he enjoyed many big moments in North London. His first Arsenal goal, for example, in August 2014 against Beşiktaş, secured a Champions League group stage place. He got a hat-trick in 14 minutes in a West Ham game in December 2016. In the 2017 Cup Final he scored the first goal — and at 229 seconds the fastest FA Cup final goal by an Arsenal player ever — in the 2-1 victory over Chelsea. There were many other similar occasions and when he left for Manchester United in January 2018 (he was swapped for Henrikh Mkhitaryan) he had scored 80 goals and made 43 assists in 166 appearances.

32 ▶ PETER STOREY

An Arsenal man through and through, Peter Storey began his career in 1961 as an apprentice right-back. He made his first-team debut in 1965 and was a regular for the next decade. He tackled hard, but was also very adept on the ball, so Bertie Mee moved him into central midfield, a position he much preferred. In 1971 it fell to Storey to face the legendary Gordon Banks and take an injury-time penalty in the FA Cup semi-final against Stoke. Happily Storey converted to make it 2-2 and keep Arsenal in the cup (they won the replay) and the chase for the Double. He left Highbury in 1977 and spent a season at Fulham before retirement.

31 ▶ EMMANUEL PETIT

Midfielder Emmanual Petit only spent three years at Arsenal, in the early days of Arsène Wenger's reign, but he made a significant impact on the field and was an important part of the 1997-98 Double-winning team. Always robust, he formed a powerful partnership with slightly younger fellow Frenchman Patrick Vieira. He had a great positional sense and although technically a defensive player, he was equally comfortable in attack. In 2000 Petit departed for the warmer weather of Spain, although after a year with Barcelona he did return to London, but to Chelsea, where he finished his playing career.

30 ▶ PIERRE-EMERICH AUBAMEYANG

In four seasons (technically three seasons and two half-seasons) Pierre-Emerich Aubameyang made 68 appearances for Arsenal and scored 92 goals, 28 of them game-winning. He arrived in January 2018 and netted on his debut against Everton, but although his time at the club was goal-laden, it wasn't exactly trophy-laden. In fact, his only trophy was the 2019 FA Cup. The final against Chelsea was played in August behind closed doors due to the Covid-19 pandemic and Aubameyang got a penalty, scored the winner and captained the team. He left the club in February 2022 for Barcelona. Although born in France, Aubameyang chose to play for Gabon and is that country's most successful player.

29 ▶ DAVID ROCASTLE

David Rocastle — or Rocky as he was to fans — was a midfielder who made 277 appearances for Arsenal and scored 34 goals. Born in South London, Rocastle was childhood friends with Ian Wright, but arrived in North London as a teenager, six years before Wrighty. He was part of the 1987 League Cup-winning team and when Arsenal won the League title in 1988-89 he played in every single match, up to and including the season's famous last game when the title was clinched at Anfield. He won another League title in 1990-91. After Arsenal he spent shortish spells at various other clubs, sadly dying from cancer in 2001 at the age of just 33.

28 ► FRANK MCCLINTOCK

Frank McLintock had the honour of captaining the 1970-71 Double-winning team. The Scotsman was signed from Leicester in 1964 for what was a club record fee of £80,000. However, his Gunners debut was inauspicious — he mis-hit a back-pass enabling John Barnwell to score for Nottingham Forest. That was bad enough, but Arsenal had sold Barnwell to buy McLintock. It took McLintock a few seasons to find his rhythm, but a switch from winger to centre-back helped, he always worked hard, and he grew into the leader's role over time. A stalwart at the club for almost a decade, he moved to Queens Park Rangers at the end of the 1972-73 season.

27 ► RAY PARLOUR

He was known as the Romford Pelé, but it was meant ironically, rather than as a compliment. Ray Parlour could certainly be somewhat error prone — he gave away a penalty in his first-team debut — but in his 15 years at Arsenal he was an extremely loyal and hard-working servant. The midfielder played under two of the great managers in the shape of George Graham and Arsène Wenger, and won three Premier titles and four FA Cups, with 1997-98 and 2001-02 being Double-winning season. He also picked up a Cup-Winners' Cup medal in 1994. He finally left for Middlesbrough in 2004 and was a far better player than he was ever given credit for.

26 ► DECLAN RICE

Worthy of inclusion in any list of Arsenal greats if only on account of those two very special free-kick goals against Real Madrid in April 2025, early on in his career Declan Rice was very much an out-and-out West Ham player. Consequently some were doubtful about his 2023 move from east to North London for a club record fee of £100 million. However, the defensive midfielder quickly demonstrated his commitment to Arsenal and tenacity on the pitch, as well as his tackling skills and instinctive reading of the game. He's also the go-to man for corners on the left, making him key to Arteta's set-piece success.

25 ► WILLIAM SALIBA

Centre-back William Saliba originally came to Arsenal from French side Saint-Étienne. That was in 2019 when he was 18. However, it wasn't until 2022, after periods on loan back at Saint-Étienne, at Nice and at Marseille, that he made his first-team debut on the opening day of the season, away to Crystal Palace. Calm under pressure, with pace and great ability on the ball, he has been a mainstay of the defence ever since. In July 2023 he signed a deal to keep him at the Emirates until 2028 and in the 2023-24 season he achieved the distinction of playing every minute of every game in the Premiership — a total of 3420 minutes.

24 ▶ DAVID O'LEARY

David O'Leary made 722 appearances for Arsenal. That is still the club record and it's hard to see it ever being bettered. He also holds the club records for the most League appearances (558) and the most League Cup appearances (70). The long-serving centre-back made his debut in 1975. He was 17 and it was a game against Burnley. His last match was the 1993 FA Cup final replay in which Arsenal beat Sheffield Wednesday 2-1 and O'Leary came off the bench in the 81st minute to replace Ian Wright. Tall, slim and speedy, he was a composed and elegant player, who won six major honours with the Gunners.

23 ▶ NIGEL WINTERBURN

A key part of Arsenal's back four in the late 1980s and 1990s, Nigel Winterburn had found success with Wimbledon before George Graham brought him to Highbury for what today seems the bargain sum of £350,000. Playing as a left-back, with Lee Dixon on the right and captain Tony Adams, with David O'Leary and then Steve Bould, in the centre, Winterburn stayed with the club into the Wenger era, winning two First Division titles, one FA Cup, one League Cup and one European Cup-Winners' Cup, plus the Double in 1997-98. In some ways an unassuming character, he was a dogged tackler, but could also pass the ball forwards with pinpoint accuracy.

22 ▶ PAT RICE

Arsenal won the Double in Pat Rice's first season. He went on to play in a total of five FA Cup finals (like David Seaman and Ray Parlour), although unfortunately only one of those — in 1979, against Manchester United — resulted in a Gunners victory. Having joined Arsenal at 15, at 18 Rice made his debut at right-back, when Peter Storey moved to midfield. Always a hard worker, he was crucial in the mid-1970s battle against relegation and became captain in 1977. He left the club in 1980 after 528 games, but returned as a coach in 1984, was briefly caretaker manager in 1996 and then assistant manager to Arsène Wenger until 2012.

21 ▶ PAUL MERSON

Paul Merson spent 12 years at Arsenal — and they were colourful ones. Always fun to watch, the attacking midfielder was a stalwart of George Graham's high-achieving late 1980s side and won the First Division title twice (1988-89 and 1990-91), the FA Cup and League Cup once each (both 1993), and the European Cup-Winners' Cup (1994). However, he was in the news for his off-the-pitch behaviour and in late 1994 he went into rehab after admitting alcohol, drug and gambling addictions. He left Arsenal for Middlesbrough in 1997, having played in 423 games and scored 99 goals across all competitions, and post-retirement has had a successful career in the media.

20 ▸ LEE DIXON

Before George Graham signed him in 1988, Lee Dixon had played for Burnley, Chester City, Bury and Stoke, but he found success at Arsenal, starting with the 1988-89 League title, famously sealed in the last game of the season against Liverpool at Anfield. A stalwart of the team's virtually impenetrable defence, Dixon played on the right, opposite Nigel Winterburn, with Steve Bould and captain Tony Adams in the centre. He went on to win another three League titles, three FA Cups and the European Cup Winners' Cup, before retiring from football in 2002 at the end of his second Double-winning season (the first being 1997-98) and becoming a media pundit.

18 ▸ EDDIE HAPGOOD

Another stalwart of the all-conquering Arsenal team of the 1930s, Eddie Hapgood was a Bristol milkman and amateur footballer. His lucky break came when Kettering Town signed him as a professional. He then got an even luckier break when Herbert Chapman brought him to Highbury. That was in 1927 and the full-back remained on the club's books until 1944. However, the Second World War effectively cut short his playing career and he served in the RAF, although he continued to play in unofficial war-time matches, both for Arsenal and England. As well as 30 caps, he won five First Division Championships and two FA Cups.

19 ▸ ALEXANDRE LACAZETTE

He arrived from Lyon and, after five years in North London, returned to Lyon, the French city of his birth. At heart, Alexandre Lacazette was a Lyon man. However, in his time at Arsenal, once he really got going he had a massive impact, making 206 appearances in all competitions and scoring 71 times. He got his first Gunners goal on his league debut — after just 94 seconds against Leicester City in 2017 — and was the club's top scorer for two seasons, in 2017-18, and 2020-21. Confident, with excellent technique and an impressive finishing ability, he also exhibited strong leadership both on and off the pitch.

17 ▸ ROBIN VAN PERSIE

Signed in 2004 from Feyenoord, where he played as a winger, Robin van Persie was bought as a potential replacement for his compatriot, Dennis Bergkamp. Under the tutelage of Arsène Wenger he developed into an excellent striker, with great ball control and an ability to read the game intelligently. Somewhat injury-prone, he could also be temperamental, particularly in his younger days, but when he was on form he was sensational, and could score with both feet and his head. In his final season at Arsenal, he netted 37 times with 13 assists. In 2012, when he left for Manchester United after eight years, he had scored 132 goals in 278 appearances.

TOP 50 GREATEST PLAYERS OF ALL TIME

16 ▶ MARTIN ØDEGAARD

He was a teenage prodigy at Real Madrid, but found it hard to establish himself. In January 2021 Arsenal became his fourth loan club and his form was transformed almost immediately. He was the club's Player of the Month that March and a mainstay of the team. He is skilful, reads the game brilliantly and has such great vision and passing ability — a goal-creating machine (he created the most chances from open play (88) in the 2023—24 Premier League season). As his work rate and leadership shone through he was made club captain at the start of the 2022-23 season and has worn the armband with pride.

15 ▶ MARC OVERMARS

Marc Overmars' debut season for Arsenal — 1997-98 — ended with the team winning the Double. It was also Arsène Wenger's first full season as manager and he took a risk in bringing the Dutchman to Highbury, because Overmars was known to be injury-prone. However, the risk paid off as Overmars flew down the wing, spearheading the counter-attack and supporting fellow countryman Dennis Bergkamp. In the event, injury took its toll in the following two seasons and he failed to have quite the same impact. His time at Arsenal was fairly short and sweet — Wenger sold him to Barcelona in summer 2000 — but he was a pleasure to watch and scored 41 goals in 142 games.

14 ▶ PAT JENNINGS

He was Tottenham's keeper for 13 years, but Spurs manager Keith Burkinshaw must have thought Pat Jennings was past it, because in 1977 he sanctioned a move across North London to Arsenal.

Jennings spent the next eight years as the first-choice keeper at Highbury. He made 327 appearances for the Gunners and won the FA Cup with them in 1979. He retired from club football in 1985, although he played his last game for Northern Ireland at the 1986 Mexico World, but it is a mark of his stand-out talent and stature that, despite the fact he switched sides, he is loved both sides of the North London divide.

13 ▶ CHARLIE GEORGE

A local lad and true Gunner, Charlie George was a potent attacking midfielder with tremendous flair. Some remember his starring role in the demolition of the great Ajax side in 1970, but more recall his goal that clinched Arsenal's first Double in the 1971 FA Cup final. There, his 111th minute shot from 20 metres flew straight into the top left-hand corner of the net. In an iconic celebration, George fell to the ground, his head, with his distinctive collar-length hair, raised and arms outstretched. Unlucky with injuries, he moved on to Derby in 1975 and then a series of other clubs.

12 ▷ CLIFF BASTIN

Cliff Bastin scored 178 goals in 395 games for Arsenal. It's some record and it stood for almost 60 years, from 1939 until 1997, when it was broken by Ian Wright (and then in 2005 Thierry Henry broke Wright's record). A member of Herbert Chapman's legendary 1930s team, Bastin was signed from Exeter City at age 17. He played as an 'outside-left' and many of those goals were scored when he picked up a through-ball provided by Alex James. He might have increased his tally further were it not for the outbreak of the Second World War. Bastin failed a hearing test and couldn't join up, but became an air raid warden and was stationed, appropriately enough, at the stadium in Highbury.

11 ▷ LIAM BRADY

Born in Dublin, Liam Brady came to Arsenal as a schoolboy, turning professional at 17, in 1973. By 1974-75 he had become a fixture in the first team and earned a reputation as one of the best attacking midfielders of his generation. The only trophy he won with the club was the 1979 FA Cup, but Alan Sunderland's last-minute winner in the final against Manchester United came out of a Brady move. Having made 307 appearances for Arsenal and scored 59 goals, in 1980 he went to play in Italy and ultimately became a manager, but he is remembered fondly in North London for being an inspirational playmaker.

10 ▷ BUKAYO SAKA

A delight to watch in full flow, Bukayo Saka's speed, dribbling and passing makes so many goals, while he scores plenty with a cool head in front of goal. Still only 23 at the start of the 2025-26 season, he joined the Arsenal Academy at seven and turned professional at 17. He made his Premier League debut in January 2019 and during 2019-20 graduated from reserve to first-team regular, although he remained on the bench when Arsenal won the 2020 FA Cup final. He was Arsenal's Player of the Season in 2021-22 and 2022-23 and was the PFA Young Player of the Year in 2023-24. Saka is an England regular demonstrating great maturity, dignity and resilience in handling racist abuse when his penalty was saved in the Euro 2020 final shoot-out.

9 ▷ FREDDIE LJUNGBERG

Super-Swede Freddie Ljungberg arrived at Highbury in 1998 as a 20-year-old, scoring within six minutes of coming onto the pitch in his Arsenal debut against Manchester United. A bundle of energy, for almost a decade he didn't stop running and always had a goal in him when it was most needed. Able to play in the middle or on either side, he was versatile and intelligent, often sitting just behind the striker, ready to pounce. He was only the third player to score in consecutive FA Cup finals — in 2001, when Arsenal lost, and in 2002, the Double year, when, of course, Arsenal won. He was also an FA Cup winner in 2003 and 2005, and a Premier League winner in 2003-04. 'We love you Freddie' went the song — and the fans certainly did.

8 ▸ DAVID SEAMAN

David Seaman was no spring chicken when George Graham signed him in 1990. In fact, he was 27, but had solid experience behind him — and a bright future at Arsenal ahead of him. He kept a clean sheet on his debut against Wimbledon and conceded just three goals in his first five games, swiftly forming a robust defensive unit alongside Lee Dixon, Tony Adams, Steve Bould and Nigel Winterburn. He was, as his nickname had it, very much a pair of 'Safe Hands', winning three league titles, four FA Cups, including the Double in 2001-02, and the 1994 European Cup-Winners' Cup. However, a year later, against Real Zaragoza in the final of the same competition, not even David Seaman could save Nayim's shot from the half-way line…

7 ▸ CESC FÀBREGAS

No matter how talented you are, if you're part of the same youth set-up as Lionel Messi you may feel you'll struggle to get a look-in. At any rate, 16-year-old Cesc Fàbregas made the momentous decision to leave Barcelona and join Arsenal. That was September 2003. Just a month later he was making his debut in a League Cup game — the youngest first-team player ever — and quickly developed into one of the world's best midfielders. Other than the 2005 FA Cup, in terms of honours it wasn't one of Arsenal's or Wenger's most successful periods, but Fàbregas was an incredible asset to the club — for example, between 2006 and 2011 he made more assists than any player in any top European league. When, after some rather drawn-out negotiations, and 57 goals in 303 appearances, he moved 'home' to Barcelona in August 2011, he was sorely missed.

6 ▸ ROBERT PIRES

Arriving in 2000 as a replacement for Marc Overmars, Frenchman Robert Pires spent six years in North London and in that time he made 284 appearances and scored 84 goals. In terms of goalscoring, his best season was 2003-04 — the 'Invincibles' season — when he hit 14 goals in the league and 19 overall. Working down the left-hand side with Ashley Cole and Thierry Henry he was masterful — many teams simply didn't know how to contain the trio — but beyond the goals he was always creative, always skilful and smart. Fans remember him as being a joy to watch — and for his habit of scoring against Spurs!

5 ▸ PATRICK VIEIRA

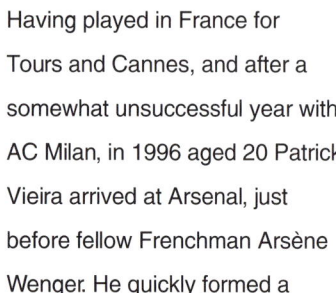

Having played in France for Tours and Cannes, and after a somewhat unsuccessful year with AC Milan, in 1996 aged 20 Patrick Vieira arrived at Arsenal, just before fellow Frenchman Arsène Wenger. He quickly formed a midfield partnership with another Frenchman, Emmanuel Petit, and was part of the team that won the Double the following season, 1997-98. Vieira's disciplinary record was sometimes poor, particularly in his early days at the club, but he epitomised the player with heart and no one ever doubted his commitment, and he was adept at both winning and passing the ball. When he finally left for Juventus in 2005, he had achieved a second Double, in 2001-02, a third Premier League title in 2003-04 and two additional FA Cup wins in 2003 and 2005.

4 ▷ IAN WRIGHT

Although famously late to the game — he didn't sign with Crystal Palace, where he spent six years, until he was almost 22 — Ian Wright more than made up for the delayed start. In his seven years at Arsenal, the club with which he is undoubtedly most identified with, he made 288 appearances and scored 185 goals, and for a time he was the team's all-time top-scorer — in 1997 he beat Cliff Bastin's record of 178, which had stood since 1939. A great striker, on the pitch he was quick, combative and always had an eye for goal, and that, combined with his effervescent personality, made him a perennial fan favourite.

3 ▷ TONY ADAMS

In Tony Adams' almost 20-year senior career with Arsenal he made 669 appearances, captained the side for 14 years and won 10 major trophies. He also had the distinction of winning League titles in three separate decades. There were low points — in 1989 the *Daily Mirror* gave him donkey's ears after he scored both goals in a 1-1 draw with Manchester United and in 1990 he went to prison for drunk-driving — but his high points included overcoming his own alcoholism and, after retirement from football, his laudable work with others dealing with addiction. He is best remembered, though, as a superb all-round defender and the exemplary leader of Arsenal's formidable 'famous back four' of the early 1990s.

2 ▷ DENNIS BERGKAMP

He just made things happen. An incredibly astute reader of the game, but with the technique and skills to execute his vision, for over a decade Dennis Bergkamp took Arsenal fans' breath away. He had initially developed his technique and skills in his native Holland, at Ajax, but after a slightly unsatisfactory spell at AC Milan he came to Highbury, where Arsène Wenger nurtured him and helped him realise his full potential. Bergkamp scored 120 goals in an Arsenal shirt, which might not sound many given how long he spent at the club and how good he was, but it was the beauty of the goals he made that turned him into a true great.

1 ▷ THIERRY HENRY

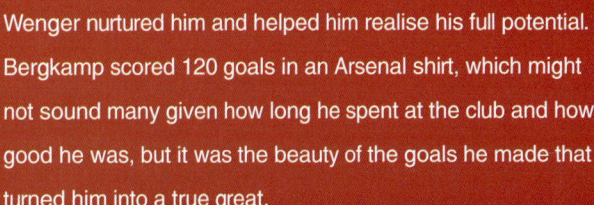
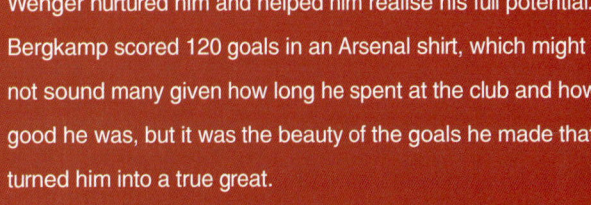

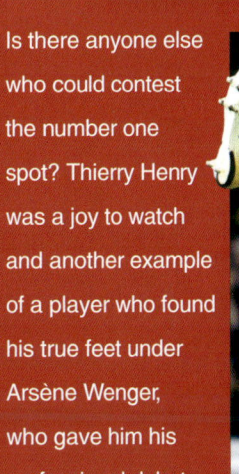

Is there anyone else who could contest the number one spot? Thierry Henry was a joy to watch and another example of a player who found his true feet under Arsène Wenger, who gave him his professional debut in 1994 when he was managing Monaco. He then brought him to Highbury in 1999. This was after Henry's short stay at Juventus, where he had played as an unsuccessful winger, but Wenger understood him and transformed him into a stylish goalscorer. Thierry Henry won two Premier League titles and three FA Cups, including one Double, with Arsenal, making 377 appearances in all competitions. In 2005 he became the club's all-time top-scorer and his total tally came to 228 goals. Ability, pace, creativity, intelligence and star quality — quite simply Thierry Henry had everything you could ever want in a striker.

TOP 5 GREATEST MANAGERS OF ALL TIME

Every new boss arrives at the Arsenal hoping to add silverware to the club's trophy cabinets. Some found instant success, while others had to wait to see the fruits of their hard work. The best of them, featured here, have been incisive tacticians, skilful man-motivators and hard taskmasters, as well as fascinating characters in their own right. These five are part of the club's rich history and their legacies will be celebrated by generations of fans to come.

▶ The greatest managers who have helped Arsenal achieve their quest to glory

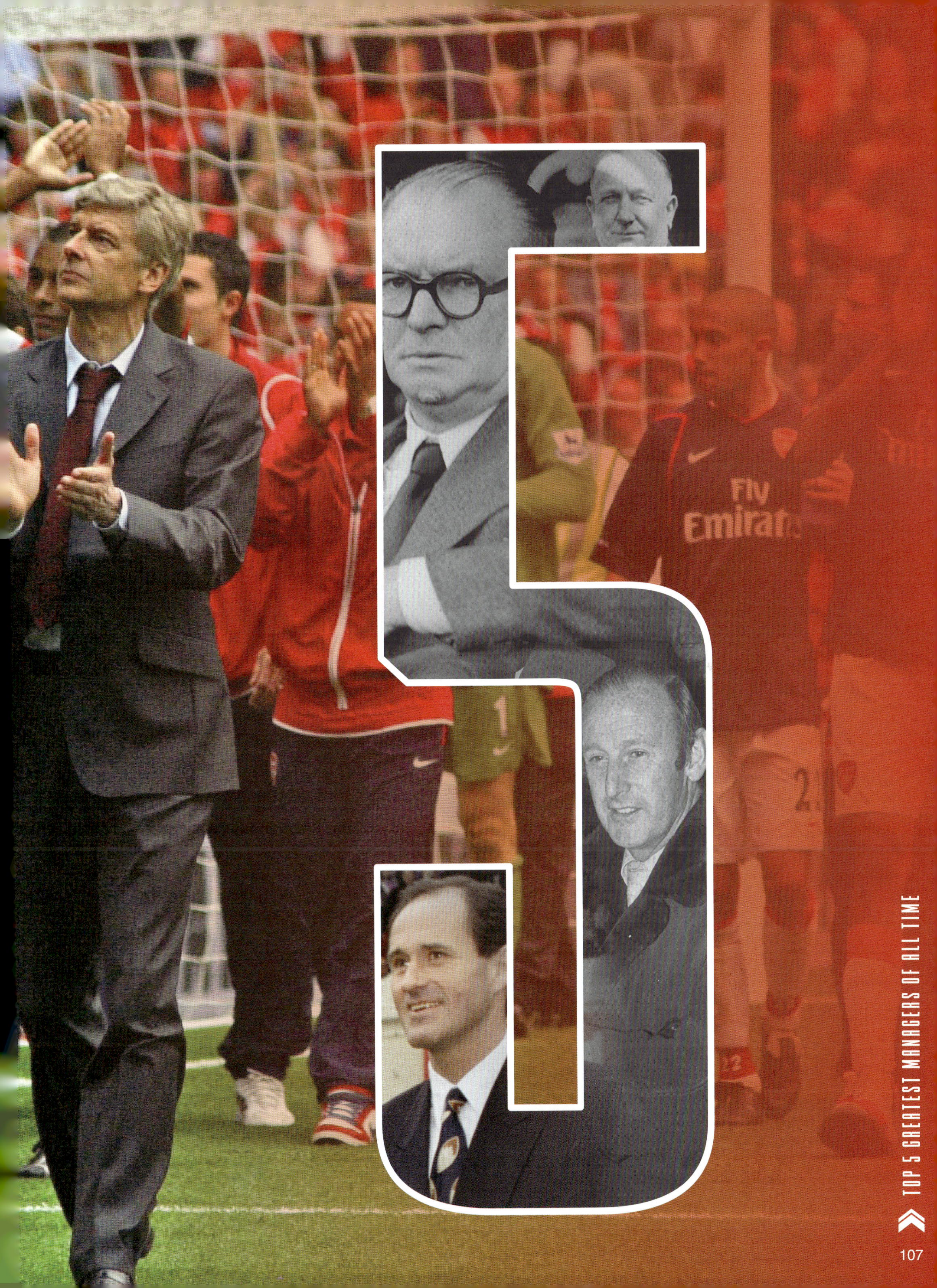

HERBERT CHAPMAN

EXTREMELY SUCCESSFUL AND REGARDED AS THE FIRST 'MODERN' MANAGER

In 1925, when Herbert Chapman arrived at Arsenal having accepted the £2,000-a-year job of manager, the club had an empty trophy cabinet and had only just avoided relegation. In those days, £2,000 was a very generous salary, reflecting Chapman's status and considerable experience in the game. It also symbolised how far he had come.

Chapman was born in Kiveton Park, a village near Rotherham in what is now South Yorkshire, in 1878. He was the son of a coal miner and went to Sheffield Technical College to study mining engineering, but what he was really interested in was football. As a player — he was an inside-forward — he played for several lower division clubs, as well as Sheffield United, but didn't make much of an impression. However, it was as a manager that he made a real and lasting impact.

In 1907 he was appointed to his first managerial role, at Northampton Town, and two years later he took the club to the Southern League title. Then, in 1912, he moved to Leeds City, where, safe to say, he swiftly put the team on the road to success until the First World War intervened and football at a national level was largely suspended. After the war, though, the club was consumed by a corruption scandal and the FA disbanded it, banning Chapman from working in football in the process. However, Chapman appealed the ban and got it lifted, successfully clearing his name.

His next stop, in 1921, was Huddersfield Town, where he went on a real winning streak, starting with the 1922 FA Cup — the final saw Huddersfield beat Preston North End 1-0 — and continuing with back-to-back First Division titles, in 1924, 1925 and 1926 (the 1926 team was ostensibly his, even though he was no longer in charge).

And so to Arsenal, who were, to be blunt, down in the doldrums at the time. He was determined to improve their fortunes, though, by convincing the board to back his vision and invest in the club, buying new players, including superb players like David Jack, Cliff Bastin and Alex James, and introducing new ideas. He began by changing the club's name from 'The Arsenal' to simply 'Arsenal', because, all other things being equal, when teams were listed in alphabetically it would put them at the top. He got the name of the local underground station changed from Gillespie Road to Arsenal, too, and he even altered the kit, pairing the red shirts with white sleeves so that they would stand out more.

Those were some of the relatively superficial changes he made, but off the field he also pioneered the use of physiotherapists and dieticians, and emphasised the importance of physical fitness. Significantly, he introduced an approach called the WM

▶ Chapman pictured in the early 1930s at the height of Arsenal's dominance. He made innovative changes to the game, on and off the pitch

formation. This involved five forwards, two midfielders and three defenders arranged in a 3-2-2-3 zigzag shape, which was flexible and gave the team creative options. It also allowed them to exploit changes to the offside rule, which had been recently brought in. He introduced floodlights to Highbury, where evening matches attracted large crowds, and argued for European club competitions to give players experience in another arena.

These innovations worked, too. In Chapman's first season with the club Arsenal reached an FA Cup quarter-final and came second in the league, their highest position to date. They got to their first FA Cup final in 1927, but lost 1-0 to Cardiff City (the only time the FA Cup has been won by a non-English club), before lifting the trophy themselves in 1930, beating Chapman's old club Huddersfield Town 2-0 in the final. They then won their first league title in 1930-31 and appeared in the FA Cup final again in 1932, losing to Newcastle 2-1. Arsenal retained their league title in 1932-33, but in January 1934, while on a scouting trip in the North, Chapman caught a cold which quickly developed into pneumonia. He died suddenly, while still in post. He was only 55.

Although there are undoubtedly managers who have won more trophies and titles than Chapman did with the Gunners, he was nonetheless a true innovator of the game and an incredibly influential figure, who laid the ground for Arsenal to become the pre-eminent team in English football throughout the 1930s — in the ten years leading up to the Second World War the team won five league titles and two FA Cups, making them indisputably the era's most successful club. Herbert Chapman is remembered in a statue that stands outside the Emirates Stadium.

Club Awards:

▶ First Division: 1930-31, 1932-33

▶ FA Cup: 1929-30

▶ FA Charity Shield: 1930, 1931, 1933

HERBERT CHAPMAN

TOM WHITTAKER

WHITTAKER

AN INNOVATOR IN THE TREATMENT ROOM AND ON THE TRAINING FIELD

Tom Whittaker served his country with distinction. Born in 1898, at the tail end of the Victorian period, during the First World War he was an ordnance engineer, working (as befitted a future Gunner) on weapons development.

In the Second World War he was an RAF squadron leader, involved in Secret Operations, and in recognition of this, particularly the missions he flew on D-Day, he was awarded an MBE. However, he served his club, Arsenal, with equal distinction.

His father was a sergeant major and he was born in an army barracks in Aldershot, Hampshire (also appropriate for a future Gunner), but at just three weeks old, the young Whittaker moved with his parents to Newcastle upon Tyne. After school he trained as a marine engineer and found employment with a Tyneside shipbuilders, where he worked until he was called up for active duty in the First World War, initially in the British Army and then the Royal Navy.

In his youth, Newcastle United fan Whittaker was a keen footballer and he continued to play for his regiment throughout the war. He even had a trial for Arsenal, but once the war ended and he was demobbed, he went back to being an engineer, until Leslie Knighton, Arsenal manager at the time, persuaded him to try his luck as a footballer instead.

He made his first-team debut in April 1920, in a 1-0 defeat away at West Bromwich Albion. Although he started out as a centre-forward and was also a useful full-back, he made the wing-half position his own and became a fixture in the team throughout the first half of the 1920s, making 70 appearances and scoring two goals. He played his last league game in March 1925, against West Ham, because in June that year he broke his kneecap while on an international tour to Australia with an FA side.

During the long recovery period, Whittaker did a course in anatomy, massage and treating injuries with electrical pulses. When he went back at Highbury he couldn't train with his teammates, but armed with his new physiotherapy qualification he helped out in the treatment room. By 1926 it was clear he wouldn't play again, so Herbert Chapman, who had taken over from Knighton as manager the previous year, made him assistant trainer.

In his autobiography, *The Arsenal Story*, Whittaker described how things weren't going Arsenal's way in a fourth round FA Cup game against Port Vale until first-team trainer George Hardy thought he'd spotted a way to solve the problem. When there was a break in play, he shouted at one of the forwards, telling him to move further up the pitch. However, Chapman, livid that his authority had been usurped, immediately ordered Hardy back to the dressing room.

On the following Monday morning, Whittaker was summoned to Chapman's office and elevated to first-team trainer on the spot. Apparently, Chapman proclaimed that he was going to make Arsenal the greatest club in the world and Whittaker the greatest trainer in the game. While pleased with the promotion, Whittaker was no doubt careful never to overstep the mark with Chapman in case he suffered the same fate as the hapless Hardy…

When Herbert Chapman died in early 1934, Whittaker and reserves manager Joe Shaw ran the team until the end of the season and clinched the league title. George Allison was then appointed to lead the club and Whittaker went back to his role as first-team trainer. He was a key part of the set-up that brought the 1934-35 and 1937-38 league titles back to Highbury, and he also acted as trainer to the England team.

Then came the Second World War, when he rose to the rank of squadron leader, but after the war ended it was back to his old job as first-team trainer. That was until 1947 when Allison resigned and Whittaker was asked to take on the manager's role. He agreed and led Arsenal to yet more league titles in 1947-48 and

▲ Tom Whittaker successfully turned from trainer at Arsenal to manager of the Gunners

1952-53, and an FA Cup win, 2-0 against Liverpool, in 1950.

Although Whittaker is by no means the most well-known manager Arsenal has ever had, he was extremely influential. A man of many talents, his knowledge and expertise on achieving peak fitness on the training field and treating injuries through physiotherapy were instrumental to Arsenal's success between the wars and in the immediate post-war period. Sadly, like his former boss Herbert Chapman, in 1956 Whittaker succumbed to a heart attack while still in post, aged 58.

Personal Awards:

▶ MBE: 1947

Club Awards:

▶ First Division: 1947-48, 1952-53

▶ FA Cup: 1950

▶ FA Charity Shield: 1948, 1953

BERTIE MEE

DISCIPLINED AND FOCUSED, HE BUILT THE TEAM THAT WON THE DOUBLE

▶ Bertie Mee wearing his customary managers' sheepskin coat, was the man in charge when Arsenal completed the Double in their historic 1970-71 season

Born in an area of Nottingham called Highbury Vale (a good omen if ever there was one), on Christmas Day 1918, Bertie Mee played as a winger for Derby County, Mansfield Town and Southampton, but his playing career was ended early by injury. However, this coincided with the start of the Second World War and Mee joined the Royal Army Medical Corps and trained as a physiotherapist. Then, after the war, he went to work in the newly established National Health Service.

Mee had kept up his football contacts, though, and in 1960 Arsenal invited him to become its physiotherapist. He spent six years behind the scenes at the club until, in 1966, he was offered the manager's job after the high-profile former Wolves and England captain Billy Wright was sacked. Mee wasn't a big name and was an unlikely choice to succeed Wright. Indeed, Mee later told the BBC that he was flattered, but surprised to be asked.

However, one of Bertie Mee's greatest strengths was that he understood his own weaknesses. He knew how to keep players fit and how to run a club, but he was less confident when it came to on-field tactics. Therefore, he immediately brought in two assistants: Dave Sexton, who would go on to manage Chelsea and Manchester United, became first-team coach, while

Don Howe, who had recently retired, having played for Arsenal and, before that, West Bromwich Albion, was put in charge of the reserve team.

Mee also excelled at developing players and he had a cohort of talented youngsters emerging from Arsenal's youth system, including Charlie George, Ray Kennedy and Pat Rice, with whom he could work, and it wasn't long before he started to make an impact on the team. In 1968 Arsenal made it to the League Cup final, but lost 1-0 to Leeds United. They reached the final again in 1969, this time losing 3-1 after extra-time to Swindon Town, with Arsenal's goal coming from Bobby Gould. Granted, the Gunners finished as runners-up in both these finals, but just getting there

finished on 65 points and secured the top spot, above Leeds in second with 64 points and some way ahead of Spurs in third with 52 points. That was on the Monday evening, but there was more to come, because on the following Saturday afternoon Arsenal were lining up against Liverpool in the FA Cup final.

In front of a 100,000 crowd at Wembley Arsenal proudly took to the field in their away kit of blue shorts and yellow shirts and socks. There was no shortage of shots from both sides, but at full-time the game was still 0-0, so it went to extra-time. Arsenal goalie Bob Wilson failed to save Steve Heighway's strike for Liverpool, but Arsenal equalised with a scrappy goal that's often credited to substitute Eddie Kelly, although TV footage shows it was George Graham who got his toe to it. Then six minutes into the second period of extra-time Charlie George slotted the ball home and not only had the Gunners won the FA Cup 2-1, they had clinched the Double as well. Arsenal were the fourth team ever to complete the elusive Double and only the second in the modern 20th century (the other being arch rivals Spurs in 1961).

Mee concluded his working life as general manager at Graham Taylor's Watford, having left Arsenal at the close of the 1975-76 season after a decade in charge. He brought discipline and attention to detail to Highbury, and was respected for it. He was a great motivator, and a great spotter and developer of talent, and Arsenal fans will always remember him as the man who delivered the Double. Bertie Mee died in 2001.

showed promise and augured well for the future.

That promise was fulfilled the following season, when Arsenal won its first European trophy and first trophy of any sort for 17 years — since 1953 — by beating Anderlecht 4-3 on aggregate to win the 1970 Inter-Cities Fairs Cup. This was despite trailing 3-0 for most of the away leg, with Ray Kennedy grabbing the sole Arsenal goal in the 82nd minute. This proved to be decisive, with Arsenal triumphing over the Belgians 3-0 on the return leg at Highbury. However, Arsenal under Bertie Mee were just getting going.

Arsenal famously won the 1970-71 league title on the last day of the season at White Hart Lane. By beating Tottenham by a solitary Ray Kennedy goal they

Personal Awards:
▶ Manager of the Year: 1971
▶ OBE: 1984

Club Awards:
▶ First Division: 1970-71
▶ FA Cup: 1970-71
▶ Inter-Cities Fairs Cup: 1969-70

GRAHAM

GEORGE GRAHAM

Born in 1944, just before the Second World War ended, in Bargeddie, just east of Glasgow in Scotland, George Graham had a tough childhood. He was the youngest of seven children and his father died of TB before he was a month old. However, his footballing talent gave him a route out of poverty to a series of clubs, starting with Aston Villa and including Chelsea, Manchester United and, of course, Arsenal. Under Bertie Mee, he scored 60 goals in 227 appearances for the Gunners and was a key member of the 1971 Double-winning side.

As a player, George Graham was a central midfielder with a light touch — his nickname was Stroller — who read the game well. Those qualities stood him in good stead in his managerial career, which began at Millwall, where he spent four successful years after he finished playing. Then, in 1986, he returned to Highbury, where he faced the challenge of revitalising a team that had been underachieving for some time, but it didn't take him too long to make a mark.

He began by disposing of most of the existing team and bringing in new signings and youth players, notably a young defender called Tony Adams and Martin Hayes, a winger who consistently scored. He also introduced some discipline to the changing room and the pitch, but whatever he did it was working,

because in Graham's first season in charge Arsenal finished fourth in the league and won the 1987 League Cup by beating Liverpool 2-1. The following year they lost 3-2 to Luton in the final of the same competition, but achieved sixth in the league.

By this point, though, Graham had astutely built his team and the famous back line of Adams as captain, Lee Dixon, Steve Bould and Nigel Winterburn was in place. It would be the foundation of the club's defence for the next ten years or so, a defence that was so efficient people criticised it as 'boring'. In this era his preferred midfield consisted of Paul Merson, David Rocastle and Michael Thomas, and upfront he had the generally reliable goalscorer Alan Smith, who netted 115 times in the course of his Arsenal career.

The battle to become 1988-89 First Division champions went right down to the wire and was one of the most dramatic in the history of English football. The last match of the season had previously been postponed due to the Hillsborough tragedy and Liverpool had already won the FA Cup when Arsenal faced them at Anfield. To take the title — and deprive Liverpool of what would have been a momentous Double — Arsenal not only had to win, but had to win by two goals.

▶ George Graham laps up the applause from his players and the delighted Highbury fans after winning another First Division title in the 1990-91 season

Club Awards:

▶ First Division: 1988-89, 1990-91

▶ FA Cup: 1992-93

▶ League Cup: 1986-87, 1992-93

▶ FA Charity Shield: 1991 (shared with Tottenham Hotspur)

▶ European Cup Winners' Cup: 1993-94

▶ Football League Centenary Trophy: 1988

Needless to say, it was a tense affair. Smith got goal number one, but it looked like goal number two would never come, until Michael Thomas finally scored in what was virtually the last minute. Graham's men had shown that they were resourceful and resilient, and they had been rewarded, which was especially sweet since it was a long ten years since they'd last won the FA Cup and 18 years since they'd won the league.

Under Graham's stewardship Arsenal claimed the league title again in 1990-91, the year when he brought goalkeeper David Seaman and the Swedish winger Anders Limpar to the club. What's more, at the beginning of the next season he had the acumen to sign one Ian Wright. His team then went on to win FA Cup in 1992-93, but the pinnacle of his achievements at the club came in 1994, when Arsenal were victorious in the European Cup-Winners' Cup, defeating Parma 1-0 in the final with a Smith goal. It was Arsenal's first

European trophy and a real feather in Graham's cap. It was also, many people say, the origin of the popular fan chant 'One nil to the Arsenal', sung joyfully, but also with a certain degree of self-awareness, because that was such a common scoreline in this period.

George Graham was manager of Arsenal for almost a decade. The reason that his tenure came to end wasn't really due to results on the pitch, but because he was found to have been involved in a financial scandal related to illegal payments from agents — so-called 'bungs' — in player transfers. The Arsenal board deliberated, but felt they had no choice but to fire him. He had filled the Highbury trophy cabinet and it was a rather sad and unfortunate end to a glittering era. He also received a one-year ban from working in football.

ARSÈNE WENGER

HIS IMPACT ON ARSENAL AND ON ENGLISH FOOTBALL WAS INCREDIBLE

Few had heard of the Frenchman Arsène Wenger when he was appointed in 1996, but by the time he left in 2018 he had transformed not only Arsenal but English football as a whole. He spent 22 years at the club and as the longest-serving manager in its history, his impact can be measured not only in the number of trophies in the cabinet, but also in the ethos of the club — and his legacy lives on under current manager Mikel Arteta, who Wenger originally brought to Arsenal as a player in 2011.

Born in Strasbourg, Alsace, on the French/German border, when he was young Wenger played for the local lower league team Mutzig. While completing an economics degree at the University of Strasbourg, he moved to Mulhouse, then ASPV Strasbourg and finally RC Strasbourg. His career as a player certainly wasn't in the upper levels of French football, but in his last couple of years at RC Strasbourg he also coached the reserve and youth teams. Via an assistant manager job at league two Cannes, this led to him being appointed manager at league one club Nancy.

Although his three years at Nancy weren't exactly triumphant, he started to develop many of the innovative ideas he would later employ at Arsenal. However, it was at AS Monaco, where he spent over seven years, that he was first able to make his

managerial mark by winning the French first division and the French Cup, the equivalent of the FA Cup. He then spent two years in Japan, managing Nagoya Grampus Eight. Before Wenger's arrival they was languishing at the bottom of the J League, but he swiftly turned them round and they won the 1996 Emperor's Cup and Super Cup.

Nicknamed 'Le Professeur', partly because of his academic appearance, but mostly because of his intelligence and innovative approach to the game, Wenger had a clear footballing philosophy. In the 21st century it has become the norm for clubs to be guided by sports science, but in the late 1990s it was

◀ Wenger was a master tactician that took the Gunners to new heights

▶ An emotional send off at the Emirates for Wenger, after more than 20 years at the helm for Arsenal

revolutionary. He placed an emphasis on nutrition and fitness, and introduced new training methods.

And his approach paid off, particularly in the late 1990s and early 2000s. In 1998, he became the first foreign manager to win the Double. Wenger and Arsenal also won the Double in 2001-02 and then there was the 'Invincibles' season of 2003-04, when the team went unbeaten in the league for 38 games and 49 games in total (the last team to do this had been Preston North End in 1888-89). Towards the later stages of his time in charge, Arsenal were always up there, but couldn't quite clinch the league title. Apart from his last two seasons — they were fifth in 2016-17 and sixth in 2017-18 — they never finished out of the top four, but competition, particularly from Chelsea and the two Manchester clubs, was fierce.

In total, Wenger won seven FA Cups with Arsenal. The first four came in fairly quick succession. In 1998 they beat Newcastle United 2-0; in 2002 they also won 2-0, but on that occasion against Chelsea; in 2003 they met Southampton and came away 1-0 victors; and 2005, when Arsenal faced Manchester United, it ended 5-4 on penalties. Nine seasons without silverware then followed, until in 2014 they brought home the FA Cup again by beating Hull City 3-2 after extra time. They made it to the Cup final again the following year, 2015, definitively beating Aston Villa 4-0, and once more in 2017 when, with Chelsea their opponents, they emerged 2-1 winners.

No doubt he felt he could have achieved more, but under Wenger's guidance Arsenal found success in Europe too. Although on both occasions they failed to win the ultimate prize, they reached the 2000 UEFA Cup final and the 2006 UEFA Champions League

final, losing on penalties to Galatasaray and 2-1 to Barcelona respectively.

Arsène Wenger transformed the way Arsenal performed. Wengerball, as it was called, meant holding on to the ball, wearing down the opposing team, and suddenly switching between defence and attack. It was important for players to stay in position and pass the ball quickly, accurately and with style, but even full-backs were invited to surge forward if the opportunity opened up, because creativity was much prized. He made a remarkable contribution to Arsenal and to honour his legacy in 2023 a statue of the great man was unveiled at Emirates Stadium.

Personal Awards:

▶ Premier League Manager of the Season: 1997-98, 2001-02, 2003-04
▶ OBE: 2003

Club Awards:

▶ Premier League: 1997-98, 2001-02, 2003-04
▶ FA Cup: 1997-98, 2001-02, 2002-03, 2004-05, 2013-14, 2016-17
▶ FA Charity/Community Shield: 1998, 1999, 2002, 2004, 2014, 2015, 2017

TOP 10 GREATEST TEAMS OF ALL TIME

The Arsenal story is full of teams who have shown passion and skill as they brought silverware and acclaim to this great club. From their first league winners in 1931 to Arsène Wenger's double-double winners and on to today's young Gunners, Arsenal have consistently produced teams with skill and substance. Definitively comparing teams from different times is an impossible task, but these ten have undoubtedly provided the glory and entertainment to secure their place in the club's history.

▶ The 'Invincibles' from 2003-04 and Tom Whittaker's league-winning Arsenal from 1953

▼ Arsenal defending against Spurs in 1988

When a moribund Arsenal needed waking up in the late 1980s, the job fell to George Graham. Moving on ageing players from Tony Woodcock to Kenny Sansom, he brought unheralded signings to join promising players from the youth academy and crafted a side full of creativity, guile, resolve and an indomitable team spirit.

Tony Adams, Martin Hayes and David Rocastle had been among the first crop of youth players to break into the first team, but they were soon joined by Michael Thomas, Paul Davis and the mercurial Paul Merson. Meanwhile, Graham's signings were considered and strategic. Striker Alan Smith and winger Brian Marwood invigorated the forward line, Kevin Richardson added grit to the midfield, while the defence was remodelled with new full-backs Lee Dixon and Nigel Winterburn joining Adams and stalwart David O'Leary.

In both the 1986-87 and 1987-88 seasons Graham's developing Arsenal had topped the table at various points, but had failed to capitalise. The manager knew they were not quite ready, although the unexpected League Cup trophy at the expense of Liverpool in 1987

was a major step. A sixth place in the league in 1987 was followed by a fourth position in 1988 and the young team needed to believe that they were the equal to the league's best teams.

When Tony Adams, still only 21, replaced Kenny Sansom as club captain in March 1988, it felt the transformation was complete and defender Steve Bould was the only major signing before the new season. Graham worked relentlessly on getting his back four to work as a unit, the midfield had steel and creativity and there were goals in Rocastle and Smith.

When Arsenal won the title in 1989, it was a team effort with just 17 players playing all season. They scored more than any team — Alan Smith hitting 25 goals — and defended resolutely, keeping 14 clean sheets. The team had limitations — they let an 11-point lead slip — but they responded to every setback. They went top on Boxing Day and kept it until the penultimate game of the season when a defeat at Highbury left them with an almost impossible task at Anfield. There, it was the defensive strength, attacking flair and most of all, the indomitable team spirit that saw them through.

A rsenal had finished the previous season in 12th position, exited both domestic cups at the first hurdle and had bought in absolutely no one in the summer — their record signing Peter Marinello, already deemed a flop. And yet, the faithful drew hope from their one success, a European Fairs Cup victory.

It was a time when football was brutal, every point was scrapped for and expressive play was scarce. Arsenal were well stocked with hard men, from skipper Frank McLintock to Bob McNab, John Roberts and Peter Storey and even 'Stroller' George Graham and Peter Simpson had plenty of bite. They also had a safe pair of hands in Bob Wilson in goal, a proven goalscorer in John Radford and a marauding winger in George Armstrong. What they lacked was flair. Fortunately, with Marinello floundering, two emerging young guns, Charlie George and Ray Kennedy came of age.

The team would earn a reputation as dull and defensive. Under the pragmatic and cautious manager Bertie Mee they certainly could be. Arsenal won 14 games by a single goal margin, including ten 1-0 victories and 25 clean sheets in 42 starts and progressed to the FA Cup final through replays in every round but one. However, as the season

▲ Arsenal players parade the European Fairs Cup at Highbury, ahead of their wonder Double season

progressed they also registered some eye-opening results: a Radford hat-trick inspired a 4-0 thrashing of Manchester United; West Bromwich Albion were hammered 6-2 and champions Everton were sent home with a 4-0 defeat.

Legend has it that George Armstrong said to his teammates, after the Boxing Day goalless draw with Southampton: 'I bet we win the Double'. In the New Year, Mee and assistant Eddie Howe's safety-first system tightened and the return of Charlie George, who had broken an ankle in the season's second match, added zip to the attack. They won nine consecutive matches from March. Despite a defeat at their only league rivals, Leeds United, Arsenal held their nerve to win the title at White Hart Lane and days later an exhausted Charlie George hit that delicious winner at Wembley. Arsenal fans were in double dreamland. Mee's team would never be celebrated for their stylish football as Tottenham Hotspur's had been ten years earlier, and they wouldn't hit those heights again — but for one glorious season they were indefatigable and all conquering.

TOP 10 GREATEST TEAMS OF ALL TIME

THE UNSTOPPABLE FORCE (1990-91)

The 1991 League Champions were not universally loved but the Highbury faithful revelled in the 'boring Arsenal' tag as George Graham's team battled (even literally) their way through the league season. With strength, spirit and a plan, even a point deduction and the enforced absence of their captain could not deny them another league title.

The team that had won the league so spectacularly two years earlier were a settled squad by the 1990-91 season. The youngsters, including striker Kevin Campbell, were now established players; the backline had coalesced into one of the most solid defences the league had ever seen and in Alan Smith they had a proven goalscorer. To this squad, Graham had added goalkeeper David Seaman and Swedish winger Anders Limpar.

A miserly defence and goals from Limpar enabled the team to settle into an unbeaten streak. The only blip was the mass brawl that followed their 1-0 defeat of Manchester United in October, for which Arsenal were uniquely deducted two points. That left them eight points behind runaway leaders Liverpool. The two unbeaten teams met at Highbury in December, where a Gunners statement 3-0 victory was inspired by the in-form Merson.

Until defeat by Chelsea in February, Arsenal registered a 23 game unbeaten streak in the league that they immediately picked up again. Even a three month absence of their imprisoned inspirational skipper, was shrugged off. Tony Adams returned for the crucial tie at Anfield in March, where Seaman repelled everything thrown at him and Merson again excelled in a memorable 1-0 victory.

Tough hopes of a double were thwarted by a semi-final defeat to Tottenham Hotspur, the Gunners league form continued unabated. The defence remained virtually watertight, while Smith and Campbell scored regularly. In the penultimate game of the season, having been crowned champions an hour before the game, a Smith hat-trick dispatched their new bitter rivals Manchester United.

Five days later, a Limpar hat-trick ignited the celebrations in a 6-1 walloping of Coventry City, the perfect response from a team who had received scant praise for their magnificent season. The 'almost invincibles' (they lost just one league match) conceded just 18 and scored a respectable 74 goals. The Arsenal faithful might have seen more skilful and exciting teams, but this squad had plenty of talent and an astonishing will-to-win.

▲ Andy Linighan, Kevin Campbell, Paul Davis, David Rocastle and Lee Dixon celebrate First Division title success for Arsenal in 1991

om Whittaker's team were rich on experience. For many of them, still smarting from the previous season's defeat in the FA Cup final and a late-season slump that destroyed their title ambitions, the 1952-53 season was possibly their last chance of silverware. They clearly had the personnel and a manager with a strong tactical plan, now could they show the staying power?

Whittaker's team had been five years in the making. It was built around a core of players from the 1948-49 title-winning season. The team captain, Joe Mercer, was a tough-tackling wing-half. Now 38-years-old, he had been on the verge of retirement since achieving that feat. Don Roper, now 30, played left wing or centre-forward and Scottish inside-forward Jimmy Logie (31) was full of creativity, the natural successor to Alex James.

The rest of the team had been carefully assembled in the late 1940s. Among them were Welsh keeper Jack Kelsey, who was breaking into the side at the expense of 46-year-old George Swindin; another Welsh international in Ray Daniel, a formidable centre-half; the powerful Scottish wing-half Alex Forbes; inside forward Doug Lishman, the club's top scorer every season from 1951 to 1955 and Cliff Holton, a

▲ Arsenal proudly displaying the First Division and Charity Shield trophies in 1953

rampaging centre-forward with a thunderbolt of a shot.

As the season progressed Arsenal and Preston North End vied for top spot: Arsenal consistently picking up useful points away from home. They won 5-1 at Anfield and secured a 3-1 victory at neighbours Tottenham Hotspur in front of nearly 70,000 spectators. Christmas Day saw an incredible 6-4 win over Bolton Wanderers at Highbury.

Belief increased as the season drew to a climax. Holton hit all four goals in a thrashing of Aston Villa and Lishman collected a hat-trick in a vital win over Stoke City with two games remaining. The first was at rivals Preston where a win would have secured the title but ended 2-0. In the season's final game against Burnley at Highbury, a win was still required. The Gunners' mettle was tested with a nine-minute deflected goal for the visitors. Undeterred, Alex Forbes hammered a 25-yard equaliser and Arsenal's attack went into overdrive. Within 30 minutes they were 3-1 up and despite conceding late, held on. They had won the league on goal difference. Pressure? What pressure?

TOP 10 GREATEST TEAMS OF ALL TIME

PROJECT ARTETA (2023-2025)

O ver five years, Mikel Arteta transformed a team that lacked direction into title and Champions League contenders. After a thrilling 2022-23 season in which the Gunners' title-challenge fizzled out, Arteta strengthened a squad already rich in young talent. He brought in goalkeeper David Raya, striker Kai Havertz and club-record signing Declan Rice, the most expensive English player ever.

The team was settled for most of the 2023-24 season. In front of Raya were full-backs Ben White and Oleksandr Zinchenko and centre-backs Gabriel and William Saliba. Rice came in as the holding midfielder with Martin Ødegaard the playmaker, while Martinelli, Havertz, and Leandro Trossard joined a fluid attack lead by Buyako Saka and Gabriel Jesus.

Notable results included a 1-0 win over Manchester City, and an incredible four weeks from February in which they scored 24 goals — thrashing Liverpool and Newcastle at the Emirates, and winning 6-0 at West Ham and Sheffield United and 5-0 at Burnley. A gutsy 0-0 draw at Manchester City and wins at Tottenham and Manchester United, showed they now had the stamina to take the title race to the end, but unfortunately had to be content with second place.

Arsenal's 89 points was only one less than garnered

▲ Arteta giving instructions as he developed a great Gunners side

by the Invincibles and would have been enough to win the title in 20 of the previous 31 Premier League seasons. Raya brought a calm to their restarts from the back, Rice provided immaculate cover, Ødegaard was majestic in his passing and Saka was devastating up front. Rice's masterful dead ball strikes paid dividends too as they hit twenty set-piece goals (16 from corners). Though more cautious than the previous season, they still scored freely; 91 goals marked a Gunners record in the Premier League.

Arsenal went out in the Champions League to an experienced Bayern Munich team, but learned a lot. The following season, while injuries contributed to them once again trailing Manchester City, basically the same team recorded famous home and away victories over Real Madrid in the Champions League quarter-finals and were desperately unlucky to be eliminated by PSG in the semi-final.

Despite the Premier League and Champions League becoming more and more competitive, Arteta's team came so close. Those 2023-2025 seasons were of the highest quality, but could there be even more to come from this young side?

ARSENAL LEGENDS

THE GREAT ENTERTAINERS (2004-2006)

How do you follow an undefeated title-winning season? Arsène Wenger's response was to set about establishing his team as the nation's great entertainers. It was a rollercoaster ride with scintillating performances, an FA Cup triumph and a Champions League campaign provided the lasting memories.

From August 2004, 'The Invincibles' carried on where they left off with their unbeaten run stretching to 49 games before a controversial penalty led to a defeat at Old Trafford and the infamous post-match 'Pizzagate' outrage. The Gunners were knocked out of their stride and never fully recovered.

Injuries, suspensions and defeats in key matches meant the Gunners failed to win the Championship. However, Wenger's team were indisputably the nation's great entertainers. They scored 15 more goals than any other team in 2004-05, with Thierry Henry accumulating 30 in all competitions. Robin van Persie announcing his arrival with an amazing stoppage-time goal at Highbury and a Dennis Bergkamp masterclass in a 7-0 thumping of Everton will live long in the memory. The strength and spirit of the squad was demonstrated by the FA Cup final win on penalties over now bitter rivals Manchester United despite missing Sol Campbell and Henry through injury and having José Antonio Reyes red-carded.

Patrick Vieira's winning penalty was his final kick for Arsenal as he left for Juventus with Cesc Fàbregas, Alexander Hleb or Mathieu Flamini trusted to fill the great man's boots. Though they clearly missed him in league games, Europe was a different matter. The Gunners set out their stall with a club record five consecutive victories in the group stage but faced tough opponents in the knockout rounds.

After Henry's wonder goal in Madrid and Jens Lehmann's heroics in the return saw off Real, the quarter-final brought Juventus. Vieira's welcome return to Highbury was overshadowed by 18-year-old Fàbregas's majestic performance and a victory that was completed by an accomplished defensive performance in Turin. In the semi-final against Villarreal, it was Gilberto and Kolo Touré's time to shine with Lehmann again to thank for an 88th-minute penalty save in Spain to see them through to the final. The disappointed of that night in Paris will never dissipate, but that young team certainly made the club proud.

With Bergkamp, Pires, Cole, Reyes and Lauren all moving on it was the end of an era, but what a time to be a fan!

▲ FA Cup winning celebrations for Arsenal in 2005, after defeating Manchester United

CARLING CHAMPIONS

This was surely the greatest Arsenal team of the 20th century. Arsène Wenger had inherited a strong squad of players from his predecessor Bruce Rioch, but by his second season the Frenchman had imprinted a style on his team that oozed class, yet also had the fighting qualities necessary to triumph in English football.

In goal, England's David Seaman was in his eighth year at the club. He had familiar faces — Dixon, Adams, Bould and Winterburn — in front of him. The best defence the Premier League had ever seen. If that was ready made then the midfield was his creation. He brought in Patrick Vieira, Emmanuel Petit and Marc Overmars and got the best from a new homegrown hero in Ray Parlour, while Ian Wright, Dennis Bergkamp and teenager Nicolas Anelka were as potent a forward line as any in the world. Injuries? No problem. Alex Manninger, Martin Keown, Gilles Grimaldi, Stephen Hughes, David Platt and Christopher Wreh all stepped up when called upon.

The season was full of memorable moments, The 13-game unbeaten run to open the season; the statement 3-2 defeat of Manchester United in November courtesy of David Platt's header seven minutes from time; Dennis Bergkamp's incredible hat-trick against Leicester City

and Ian Wright securing his record as the club's greatest ever goalscorer.

From 13-points adrift in sixth place, Arsenal went unbeaten from Boxing Day until they won the title with two games remaining. An emphatic 3-1 home victory over Newcastle United gilded by a 30-yard Vieira rocket saw them close the gap to Manchester United to four points and with a 5-0 thrashing of Wimbledon they went to the top of the table.

They won the title beating Everton 4-0 capped by Steve Bould sending Tony Adams through to score a one-on-one: an iconic moment in the club's history. Of course, the Gunners weren't finished there. An FA Cup triumph over Newcastle United at Wembley landed them the club's second Double.

Gary Neville named Arsenal's class of '98 as the best English side he faced in his career. 'That 1998 Arsenal team had everything,' he said. 'Pace, power, strength, great defenders, a good goalkeeper and good finishers. That was a complete team.'

▲ Arsenal in 1998 as League Champions. It was a second Double glory for the Gunners, also winning the FA Cup

▼ An ever growing set of trophies for Arsenal in 1932

n November 1934, England played Italy in an International match at Highbury. The England side included seven Arsenal players. Such was the calibre of the team, which also featured Scottish and Welsh internationals. Herbert Chapman had died ten months earlier, but this was testament to the team that he built through the early 1930s.

Through this era the spine of the team remained consistent. In goal was Frank Moss, signed from Preston in 1931. The defensive positions were occupied by England skipper Eddie Hapgood and George Male with the no-nonsense Herbie Roberts at the newly created centre-half position. Half-backs were veteran Welshman Bob John and the ferocious tackling Scot, Frank Hill, while a forward line featured the playmaker Alex James, nifty winger Joe Hulme and prolific goalscorers in Cliff Bastin and David Jack.

Although a handful of these players helped Arsenal to their first Championship in 1931, the 1932-33 title-winning season, the first in which Arsenal wore their now famous red shirts with white sleeves, was the flowering of Herbert Chapman's project at the club. A combination of innovative tactics and coaching and

the finest players available made Arsenal the greatest team in the land. They won in the following season too, despite the club being rocked by the sudden death of Herbert Chapman in January 1934.

George Allison was appointed manager as Arsenal attempted to win a hat-trick of titles, and bolstered the side with the signing of Bill Crayston, a tough right-half; England half-back Alex Copping, the original hard man; and Ted Drake the finest centre-forward of the inter-war years. Drake hit a hat-trick in the opening home game, an 8-1 thrashing of Liverpool which was inspired by the magic of Alex James. That season they would hit eight on three occasions and seven against Wolves.

Through the first half of the season the Gunners scored freely, but lost five games, including the away tie at Sunderland, their rivals for the title. By the New Year the defence had tightened recording ten clean sheets by the end of the season. March saw a crucial 0-0 draw with Sunderland and a 6-0 win at Tottenham (their biggest ever margin of their North London rivals) in which winger Alf Kirchen, another new signing, bagged two. The Gunners never looked back, finishing four points clear of Sunderland and achieving the monumental hat-trick.

They are still called the 'Invincibles'; a team who went a record 49-games unbeaten, including a whole Premier League campaign. And yet, even that nickname sells this team short. They were simply capable of steamrollering any team with speed, elegance and scintillating football. A club once labelled 'boring' or 'lucky', had a new image. Arsène Wenger's team changed Arsenal forever.

This team was the pinnacle of the eight years that the Frenchman had so far spent at the club. The previous season he had said his side would remain undefeated through the league campaign: his prediction was a year early, but he knew… German keeper Jens Lehmann was the only major addition to the team for the 2003-04 campaign, slotting in behind defenders Ashley Cole, Sol Campbell, Kolo Touré, Lauren or Martin Keown. They were all strong but technically skilful players and, like all Wenger defences, impeccably well drilled as a unit. In front of them, patrolled Patrick Vieira, a tackler supreme and the underrated Gilberto Silva.

The security given by this mighty defence was integral to the scintillating attacking football played by the Gunners that season. Ingenuity and creativity was everywhere, but most tellingly at the feet of Freddie Ljungberg, Robert

▲ Premiership Champions for what is considered one of the greatest Arsenal teams of all time – the 'Invincibles'

Pires and Dennis Bergkamp. Spearheading this was the lightning pace and instinctive scoring ability of striker Thierry Henry at the top of his game.

Such was the confidence and ability of the team, though, players were able to swap positions and attacking strategies to devastating effect. They had intelligence as well as skill and could switch from relentless attack to determined defence. Their resolute togetherness shone through: seven times they had to come from behind and yet, they never trailed in the final 20 minutes of any of the 49 games they remained unbeaten.

To win the league in such a manner, with such style was an incredible achievement and will live forever in the record books and the memories. The season had so many glorious moments. Robert Pires' curling shot from distance in an early win at Anfield; going 1-0 down at Stamford Bridge and coming back to win in scintillating style: a Henry masterclass as he hits four in a 5-0 trouncing of Leeds United; the dogged resilience that earned a draw in the Battle of Old Trafford and winning the title at White Hart Lane.

Runners-up in the FA Cup and the Premier League the previous season, the Gunners stepped up to win their second double in four years. They played possession football with a free-flowing panache and attacked with speed, prowess and potency. They also knew that results were everything and they defended with pure grit and courage.

After an inconsistent early season, a home defeat to Newcastle United in December was Arsenal's turning point. In the next match, a gutsy performance saw them win 2-1 at Anfield despite playing with ten men for an hour. They would not lose a league game again that season. The understanding between new signing Sol Campbell and Tony Adams (in his final season) grew and Ashley Cole reached new heights; Patrick Vieira was majestic and up front Dennis Bergkamp, Sylvain Wiltord, Freddie Ljungberg, Robert Pires and Thierry Henry, in imperious form, were often unstoppable.

Two Highbury victories over Chelsea and Middlesbrough, both from behind, sent the Gunners to the top of the table at the end of the year and soon win followed win. Dennis Bergkamp's unforgettable flick, swivel and finish saw off high-flying Newcastle at St James' Park, Robert Pires, whom Wenger described as the 'oil in the engine' of that team, scored a goal of outrageous impudence to seal another crucial victory at Villa Park, while the Ljungburg and Henry's blistering goalscoring form helped turbo-charged a run of 13 consecutive victories to the end of the season.

Hard-fought victories were achieved over Liverpool and Newcastle in a journey to the FA Cup final at Cardiff. There, against Chelsea, a magnificent run and curling shot from the flame-haired Ljungburg and a sumptuous shot from Ray Parlour secured the first trophy. Meanwhile, the league came to a head at Old Trafford where the Double was secured with a cut-throat counter-attack that saw Wiltord convert a rebound from Ljungburg's shot.

Arsène Wenger's team won the league with a seven-point margin, remained unbeaten away from home and achieved a unique record of scoring in every league game. The win marked a second Double for Arsène Wenger, who was named Manager of the Year as Arsenal players swept the board. Freddie Ljungberg was Player of the Year, Robert Pires was awarded the Football Writers' Association Footballer of the Year, while Thierry Henry collected the Premier League Golden Boot.

▲ A brilliant second Double for Arsène Wenger, as he and Tony Adams display the silverware in 2002

TOP 10 GREATEST TEAMS OF ALL TIME

TOP 10 GREATEST GAMES OF ALL TIME

F rom Highbury to Real Madrid's Bernabéu
Stadium, Arsenal have been involved in
so many great performances through the
years. Each generation of Gooners have their
own favourites from triumphant cup finals
to landmark European ties to victories over the
bitterest of rivals. The following feature some of
the best of these, celebrating the brilliant individual
displays, magnificent team efforts and momentous
achievements that thrilled and excited fans and
helped build the club's peerless reputation.

▶ Michael Thomas seals victory for Arsenal against
Liverpool in the 1988-89 nail-biting First Division decider
and a jubilant Thierry Henry after finishing off Inter Milan
in 2003

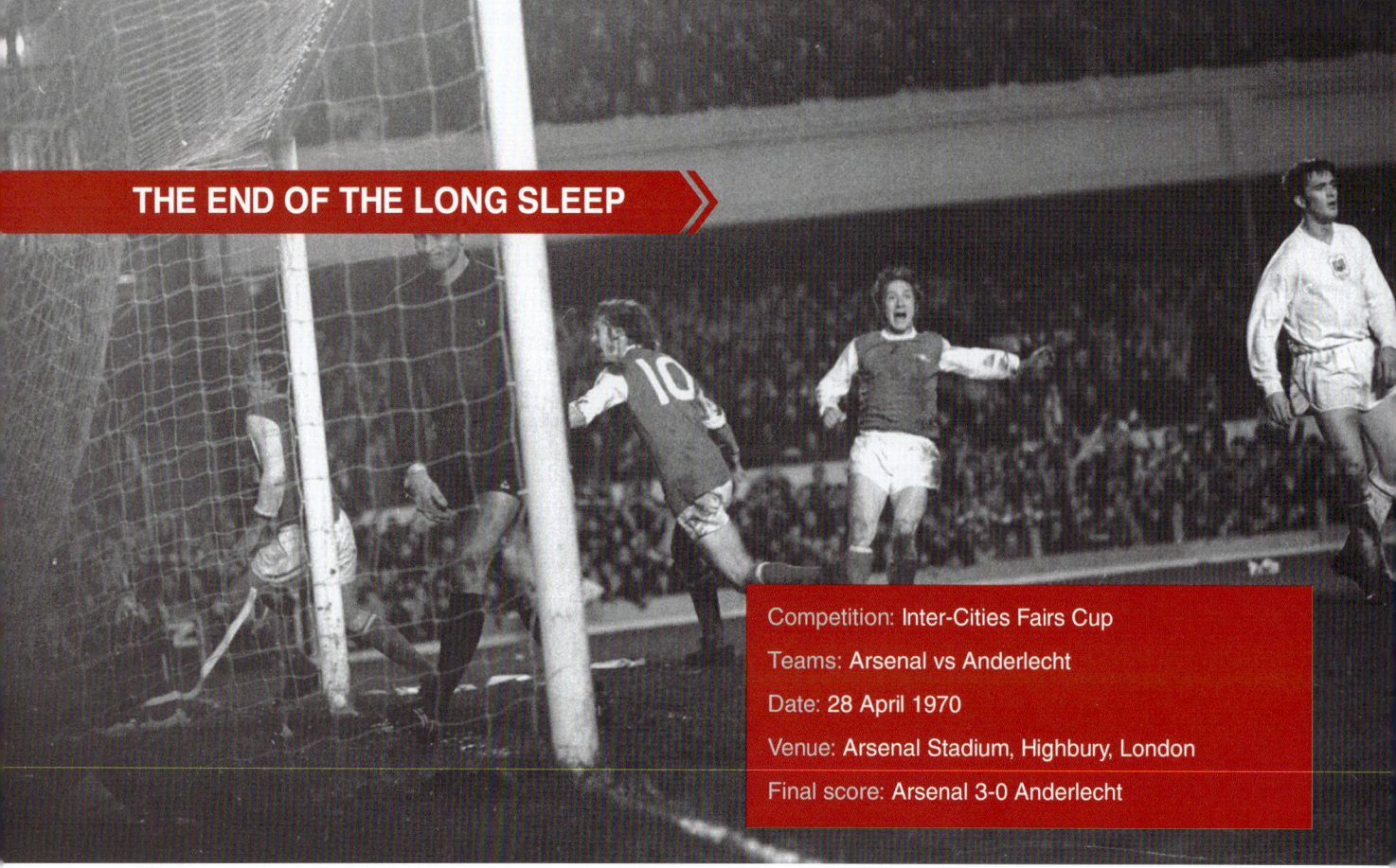

THE END OF THE LONG SLEEP

Competition: Inter-Cities Fairs Cup

Teams: Arsenal vs Anderlecht

Date: 28 April 1970

Venue: Arsenal Stadium, Highbury, London

Final score: Arsenal 3-0 Anderlecht

For the Arsenal faithful, the 1970 Fairs Cup Final presented an opportunity to end a 17-year trophy drought. With faith in Bertie Mee's side, over 50,000 fans packed into Highbury to see the Gunners produce memorable performance to win their first ever European trophy with a comeback for the ages.

Arsenal had endured a disappointing 1969-70 season, finishing 12th in the league and exiting the FA Cup at the first hurdle. However, Europe, in the form of the Fairs Cup (which evolved into today's Europa League), had been a different story. The Gunners had marched through the competition, including defeating Ajax and the inspirational Johan Cruyff in the semi-final. However, in the first leg of the final in Belgium, Arsenal were completely outplayed by a dominant Anderlecht, succumbing to a 3-1 defeat with only a late goal by young substitute Ray Kennedy giving them any chance back in London.

That didn't prevent the Arsenal fans filling Highbury and creating an incredible atmosphere. On a muddy quagmire of a pitch, Arsenal relentlessly attacked and after 25 minutes it finally paid off. At the Clock End, Geordie Armstrong's corner ended up at Frank McLintock's feet. He slid the ball back out to Eddie Kelly who beat his marker before planting a shot through the crowded area into the net from all of 20 yards.

The Gunners still trailed 3-2 on aggregate at half-time, but they had momentum and Kennedy's valuable away goal in the bag. Attacking the North Bank, they continue the spirited display as the time ticked away. There was just 15 minutes left when Bob McNab sent over a long cross to find John Radford rising to nod home at the far post. Just 90 more seconds elapsed before a Charlie George pass found Jon Sammels, who unleashed a superb diagonal shot into the bottom right corner.

Arsenal kept their 3-0 lead intact to see out a 4-3 aggregate win. The final whistle was met with scenes of jubilation, as fans hoisted their trophy-carrying skipper on their shoulders. What they had called 'The Long Sleep' was over and a glorious era was about to begin.

▲ John Radford (left of goalpost) scores for the Gunners at Highbury in the Fairs Cup Final, 1970

THE GRAF ZEPPELIN CUP FINAL

▼▲ Hovering above Wembley the Graf Zeppelin airship was not too distracting for Arsenal, as they beat Huddersfield Town in the 1930 FA Cup

Herbert Chapman had left Huddersfield Town to manage Arsenal, claiming it would take him five years to build a winning team at his new club. In 1930 — five years after his arrival — Arsenal were on the brink of fulfilling the prophecy as they faced his old club in the FA Cup Final at Wembley Stadium in search of their first ever trophy.

Arsenal, dubbed the 'Bank of England club' for their expensive signings, had yet to click. They had finished 12th in the league despite fielding top stars in David Jack and winger Alex James, alongside their season's top scorer Jack Lambert, 20-year old outside-left Cliff Bastin and 22-year old Eddie Hapgood, who was beginning to make his name as an accomplished full-back. Arsenal had lost their only other FA Cup final three years previously, and now was the time for Chapman's team to step-up.

Chapman's tactical philosophy of resolute defence and sharp forward play was evident in both teams as their centre-halves joined the defence and inside-forwards dropped back in the W-M formation that he had perfected. It was Arsenal though, inspired by Scotland's James, who were on the front foot from the outset. Legend has it that he had said to Bastin before the match: 'If we get a free-kick in their half early on, I'll slip it out to you on the wing. You give it me back and I'll have a crack at goal.' On 16 minutes, that was exactly what occurred. The winger took a quick free-kick 40-yards out, received the one-two and shot home from the edge of the area.

While James was a constant menace, half-back Bob John brilliantly patrolled the defence and linked with the forward play. Absorbed by the game, the huge crowd who had failed to notice the massive German airship the Graf Zeppelin above them, were suddenly stunned to silence as it silently skimmed the top of the stands. Huddersfield constantly attacked but found no cracks in the Gunners defence and keeper Charlie Priddy held firm. Then, with minutes to go, James sent a long ball to Lambert. The forward drew the Huddersfield keeper out and coolly slid it past him. Arsenal had won the cup and the club's first ever major trophy.

Competition: FA Cup

Teams: Arsenal vs Huddersfield Town

Date: 26 April 1930

Venue: Wembley Stadium, London

Final score: Arsenal 2-0 Huddersfield Town

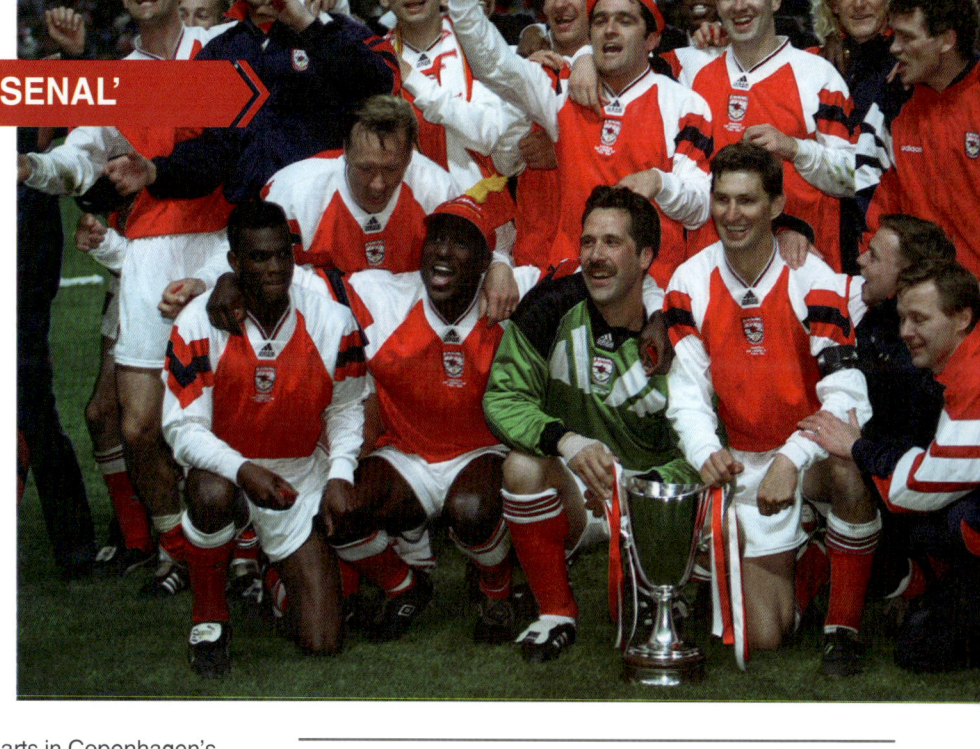

'ONE-NIL TO THE ARSENAL'

This was a match that could have been designed for George Graham's Arsenal. Few gave his depleted side much of a chance against the cup holders Parma, a team full of flair players, but they reckoned without the finest back four of the era and the indomitable spirit he had built at the club.

Arsenal fans vastly outnumbered their Italian counterparts in Copenhagen's Parken Stadium. But that was where the Gunners pre-match advantage finished. In their first European final for 24 years, George Graham's team was missing not only their talisman Ian Wright (suspended after a rash booking in the semi-final against PSG), but also the injured Martin Keown, John Jenson and David Hillier. Meanwhile Parma fielded a talented team that included Swedish star Tomas Brolin, Colombia's mercurial striker Faustino Asprilla and Italian legend Gianfranco Zola.

A frantic start to the game brought the expected onslaught from the Italian team. Only a superb last-ditch tackle from Steve Bould prevented Asprilla from an opening minute strike, then Brolin hit the post and Asprilla forced a world-class save from Seaman. Not that Arsenal were completely under siege. Kevin Campbell went close with a header from Paul Merson's corner, and Paul Davis's free-kick met by Tony Adams required a desperate clearance.

Parma continued to dominate, but it was Arsenal who took the lead with another rare attack. A mishit overhead clearance fell to Alan Smith on the edge of the area. He chested the ball down and when it bounced nicely, he hit a half-volley with his left foot off the post and in. 'One nil to the Arsenal' rang out around the stadium and for the next

▲ Arsenal with the 1994 Cup-Winners' Cup

70 minutes that chant never stopped.

The Italian side were creative, skilful and incisive with their attacks but nothing could break the red wall. The young reserves Ian Selley and Steve Morrow provided formidable cover for a back four of Lee Dixon, Steve Bould, Tony Adams and Nigel Winterburn, who were at their tenacious best, tackling and blocking nearly everything Parma could throw at them. On the rare occasions that they breached that defence, an in-form David Seaman was equal to anything they could muster.

As Tony Adams raised the trophy, a suited Ian Wright danced on the sidelines. He would have his day, but this superb victory was all about the heroic defence of that famous one-nil scoreline.

Competition: European Cup-Winners' Cup Final
Teams: Parma vs Arsenal
Date: 4 May 1994
Venue: Parken Stadium, Copenhagen
Final score: Parma 0-1 Arsenal

ARSENAL LEGENDS

A SHIFT IN POWER

Arsenal might have twice won the league title at North London rivals Tottenham's White Hart Lane stadium, but the 2002 victory at Old Trafford was momentous as well as deeply satisfying. When it mattered, a characteristic Wenger-era performance full of steel and style saw them secure their third Double at the home of their fiercest and most dangerous opponents.

Just five days after securing the FA Cup with a 2-0 victory over Chelsea, Arsenal travelled to Old Trafford for a vital fixture. The Gunners needed a draw to become Premier League champions and take the Double for the third time, while a defeat would see United take the race to the final game of the season.

Arsenal, seriously hampered by the absence of Thierry Henry, Dennis Bergkamp and Tony Adams, all injured after the cup final victory, faced a fired up United. A frantic opening 45 minutes was goalless with the home side's tackling as late as their title tilt and fortunate not to see at least one red card.

Despite their domination, the Londoner's defence remained resolute while in midfield, Edu matched the aggression and runs of Roy Keane and Patrick Vieira kept Juan Sebastián Verón in his pocket. When Arsenal won the ball, FA Cup goalscorers Ray Parlour and Freddie Ljungberg upped the tempo and created chances.

Ten minutes had elapsed when the tactics proved fruitful. Parlour robbed the ball on the halfway line and slipped it to Silvain Wiltord. The Frenchman carried the ball into the United half before sliding a clever ball to Freddie Ljungberg on the edge of the area. A fortunate bounce gave the Dane a view of goal and when Schmeichel could only parry his shot there was Wiltord, who had kept running and was perfectly placed to tap home.

The goal maintained the Gunners' record of scoring in every league game and, after defending the lead without a scare through to full time, meant they had

remained undefeated in every away game that season. They had won the league and cup double for the second time in four years, and done so at their closest opponent's ground. Arsène Wenger celebrated a 'shift in power' and the temperature of the rivalry that was about to rise to boiling point.

▲ Freddie Ljunberg and Phil Neville tussle for the ball at Old Trafford, in their nail biting title deciding fixture, 2002

Competition: **Premier League**

Teams: **Manchester United vs Arsenal**

Date: **8 May 2002**

Venue: **Old Trafford, Manchester**

Final score: **Manchester United 0-1 Arsenal**

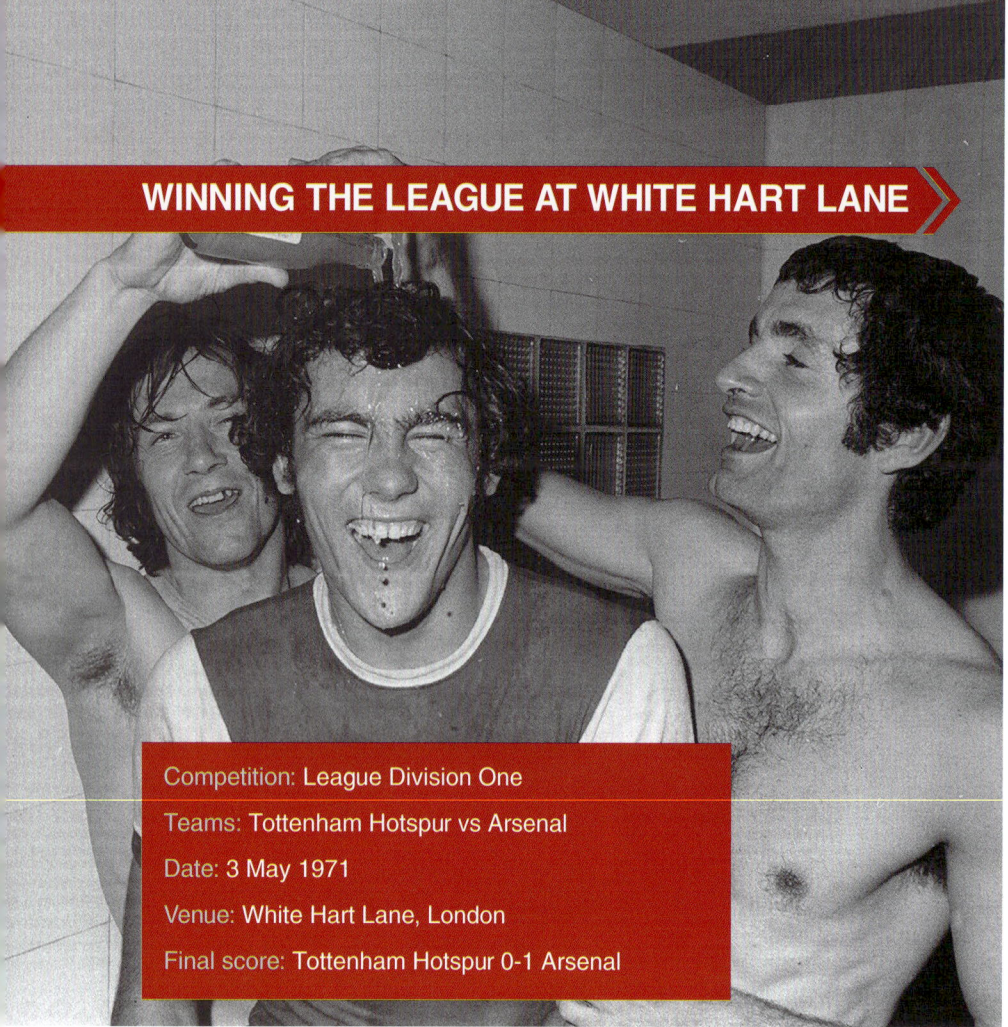

Competition: League Division One

Teams: Tottenham Hotspur vs Arsenal

Date: 3 May 1971

Venue: White Hart Lane, London

Final score: Tottenham Hotspur 0-1 Arsenal

When Arsenal ventured up the Seven Sisters Road for the last game of the 1970-71 season, it was with expectation and trepidation. There were 60,000 spectators (mostly in red and white) in the White Hart Lane stadium, 50,000 locked out and listening to the radio on Tottenham High Road. It was a night to remember for a generation of Arsenal fans for whom this victory was as good as it could get.

It was on a knife-edge. Leeds United were top of the league with 64 points having finished their League programme. Arsenal needed to win or draw 0-0 at their rival's ground to deprive Leeds of the Championship. It was certainly no forgone conclusion. Spurs, though mid-sixth in the table, were more than capable of spoiling the

party for the Gunners.

Such was the support in the stadium, it felt like a home game for the Arsenal. The roar that greeted Frank McLintock and his men was deafening. It had barely died down when Charlie George almost snatched the lead in the opening seconds with a shot only just saved by Pat Jennings. Tottenham were up for the match too and soon a Martin Peters shot clipped the bar with keeper Bob Wilson hopelessly stranded out of position.

McLintock was an inspirational general though, marshalling his team brilliantly. Arsenal began to dominate. Eddie Kelly, a late selection for the injured Peter Storey, was running the show and Geordie Armstrong ran tirelessly on the wing. As half-time approached McLintock saw a header hooked off the line and Arsenal put on pressure with a series of corners, but the all-important goal evaded them.

Tottenham came back at the Gunners in the second half: a goalmouth scramble left Wilson needing treatment and Spurs' Alan Gilzean missed a golden opportunity with a header. As each minute passed, the tension ramped up further. It was unbearable. Then, with just four minutes remaining, Armstrong gathered a loose ball and clipped in a cross to Ray Kennedy. The 19-year old rose to head the ball home from 12 yards. The stadium erupted and the noise was unabated until the final whistle. Arsenal had secured their first league title for 19 years and had won it at their Tottenham's own ground. Just five days later they would also equal their bitter rival's record of winning a League and Cup double.

▲ Ray Kennedy gets a soaking from George Armstrong (left) and Frank McLintock after the Spurs victory

THAT NEVER-TO-BE FORGOTTEN NIGHT AT ANFIELD

t was the greatest ever climax to a title race in England; a seemingly impossible dream played out before the eyes of millions on TV. On an unforgettable evening in Anfield, commentator Bryan Moore's words as Michael Thomas bore down on goal went down in history: 'It's up for grabs now!'

Arsenal travelled to Liverpool for the final match of the 1988-89 season. Their task was simple: they had to win by two clear goals to steal the title from their hosts. The emotions of the Hillsborough tragedy just six weeks before were still raw, but Liverpool had rallied admirably, winning their last four league matches convincingly. Meanwhile, Arsenal had faltered, drawing their final home game 2-2 with Wimbledon. The *Daily Mirror* headline of the 26th said it all: 'You Haven't Got A Prayer, Arsenal'.

Manager George Graham plumped for caution rather than all-out attack. However, his aim to try to catch Liverpool with a counter-attack was blunted by equally restrained tactics from the home side. The first half was cagey with few clear-cut chances. Despite the feeling that the title was slipping away fast, Graham held his nerve and his half time team talk reiterated the message 'stay patient'.

Eight minutes after the restart, an unmarked Alan Smith got the faintest of glances to a Nigel Winterburn free-kick that floated past a static Bruce Grobbelaar. The Gunners

had a lifeline. With the home side looking nervous, Arsenal hustled and pressed them at every opportunity, but to no avail. As the ninety-minute mark passed, John Barnes made for the corner and the game seemed lost.

Tony Adams hadn't given up. He won the ball and passed back to keeper Lukic. Instead of hoofing it, Lukic threw it to Lee Dixon who hit it upfield. Alan Smith controlled it brilliantly, span and played a ball to Michael Thomas sprinting through from midfield. Thomas's first touch ricocheted off his marker and back into his path. He was on the edge of the area and through on goal. By the time he reached the penalty spot, Bryan Moore has uttered his iconic exclamation and within a second Thomas has dinked it past the oncoming Grobbelaar. It was the most incredible finale in league football and according to some, revitalised football from the doldrums.

▲ A moment of magic for Michael Thomas as he puts the Gunners into a two goal lead against Liverpool

Competition: **League Division One**

Teams: **Liverpool vs Arsenal**

Date: **26 May 1989**

Venue: **Anfield, Liverpool**

Final score: **Liverpool 0-2 Arsenal**

In trouble in Europe, Arsenal needed their high-flying team to step up at the intimidating San Siro stadium in Milan. As Thierry Henry proved he was one of the world's greatest strikers, he inspired the team to a famous victory and Arsenal's greatest ever Champions League performance.

In the 2002-03 season Arsenal may have been dominant in the league with 10 wins from 13 games, but their Champions League campaign had floundered. After a 3-0 loss to Inter Milan at Highbury and a 2-1 defeat in Kyiv, Arsenal were in deep trouble in the group stage. They travelled to the San Siro for the away tie with Inter needing a result to keep their Champions League hopes alive and found themselves without key players in Patrick Vieira, Sylvain Wiltord, Martin Keown and Lauren.

The Italian side that included Cannavaro, Zanetti, Vieri, Martins began the game as they had finished at Highbury looking dangerous in attack. However, after some rough early challenges, Thierry Henry stirred. He received the ball from Robert Pires, exchanged passes with Ashley Cole and stroked home from the edge of the area with devastating accuracy. Despite the Gunners then taking complete control, a freak goal — a looping deflection off Sol Campbell — brought the home side level before half-time.

The second half was all about a certain Henry masterclass. After just three minutes, the Frenchman tormented two defenders on the left before sliding the ball across to Freddie Ljungberg whose sharp control enabled him to shoot past Inter keeper Toldo. He was a constant menace but with the scores still close with 10 minutes remaining, Arsenal needed another goal. It came from an Inter corner as skipper-for-the-day Ray Parlour's header finding Henry in his own half. He ran all the way to the host's penalty area, paused, then beat Zanetti twice before powering a shot home. He wasn't finished yet. This time on the left his cross ends up at Edu's feet for a simple finish. 4-1 to the Arsenal. Leaving the pitch to a great ovation from the travelling fans, he had hardly sat down on the bench when his replacement, Jérémie Aliadière teed up Pires for a remarkable 5-1 victory. It was the Milan club's heaviest home defeat in 47 years of European football.

▲ With the help of an inspired Henry, Arsenal eventually scored five goals demolishing Milan

Competition: Champions League
Teams: Inter Milan vs Arsenal
Date: 25 November 2003
Venue: San Siro, Milan
Final score: Inter Milan 1-5 Arsenal

I t was the greatest match the Arsenal faithful had witnessed since the club moved into the Emirates. The atmosphere in the stadium for the quarter-final first leg was incredible as the fans ear-splitting songs echoed Mikel Arteta's entreaties to 'Make it Happen'. On the field, his team did just that, exceeding all expectations, they humbled the tournament's greatest name.

Real Madrid's experienced star-studded team, Kylian Mbappé, Vinícius Júnior, Jude Bellingham and Luka Modrić among them, were always going to be tough opposition. Gunners' fans knew though, that when Arteta's team got it right, they were unstoppable. This evening Arsenal got everything right. Taking their energy from the crowd and never letting up; outplaying their regal opponents and overcoming an obstinate goalkeeper with world-class goals, they made it a night to remember.

The first half was engrossing. At first it was cagey, but slowly Arsenal took a grip on the play. Declan Rice and Thomas Partey dominated midfield as Bukayo Saka causing chaos on the wing. Courtois in the Madrid goal twice performed heroics to keep out Rice and Martinelli, while Mbappé squandered a chance that showed the visitors were still a threat.

Few expected Arsenal could step it up further in the second half. Yet, pushing further forward, with even more intensity, they overran their galáctico opponents.

▲ Declan Rice free kick heroics as he scores the first of his two goals against Euro Kings Real Madrid

Then, just 12 minutes after the break, came a moment of magic as Declan Rice curled a free-kick around the wall, and into bottom right corner of the goal. The Arsenal pressure continued unabated and on 70 minutes, Rice did it again. A man who confessed to never having scored from a free-kick before that night, whipped an even better dead ball past Courtois. When makeshift forward Mikel Merino then swept in a third goal in 15 minutes, the Emirates crowd were in dreamland.

This was the pinnacle of Arteta's team: defensively tight, controlled in possession and deadly in attack; a blend of young stars like 18-year-old Myles Lewis-Skelly stepping up and expensive signings such as Rice delivering in style and an indefatigable team spirit. It was a scintillating performance that left the Emirates crowd salivating and excited for the future.

Competition: **Champions League**
Teams: **Arsenal vs Real Madrid**
Date: **26 March 2025**
Venue: **Emirates Stadium, London**
Final score: **Arsenal 3-0 Real Madrid**

THE INVINCIBLES TAKE THE TITLE

Thirty-three years after Arsenal won the title at White Hart Lane, they returned to do it again. Unbeaten in the league, Arsène Wenger's side had already all but won the title, but to repeat the feat in style at their neighbour's home was the icing on the cake.

On the morning of the North London Derby, Arsenal sat proudly at the top of the Premier League. They had played 34 matches, won 24, drawn 10 and lost absolutely none. They were 10 points clear of second place Chelsea, who had lost their early-kick-off match, meaning the Gunners needed just one point to claim the title. What better place to do it than White Hart Lane.

Was it ever in doubt? A rampant, unbeaten Arsenal against a struggling Spurs side? If a third minute corner for the home side caused a flutter of doubt for the travelling support, it was soon assuaged — with some style. Thierry Henry picked up the ball from a loose header and ran deep into the opponents half before sliding it down the line to Dennis Bergkamp. His inch perfect cross was met by Patrick Vieira, who had run the length of the pitch to tap home. By 35 minutes the Champions-elect were two goals to the good. The second goal as sublime as the first. A mesmerising series of passes, Robert Pires to Bergkamp, Bergkamp to Vieira, Vieira to Pires was capped by the coolest of finishes from the Frenchman.

Tottenham gave it a go in the second half and an added-on-time equaliser through a Robbie Keane penalty gave the home fans something to cheer. The point required for the crowning of the champions though, was still safely secured. The Arsenal players ran to their supporters in the Park Lane end and joined in their ecstatic celebrations. All but Sol Campbell who, still bitterly resented for his betrayal of his childhood club, sensibly sought the sanctuary of the dressing room until the home fans had dispersed.

That season Arsenal fans revelled in the play of one of the most thrilling sides ever, while history books recorded the 'Invincibles' unbeaten season. For many though, winning the league at their rivals home — yet again — would be the enduring memory of a golden era.

▲ Sealing the League title at White Hart Lane — perfect!

Competition: Premier League

Teams: Tottenham Hotspur vs Arsenal

Date: 25 April 2004

Venue: White Hart Lane, London

Final score: Tottenham Hotspur 2-2 Arsenal

MAKING HISTORY AT THE BERNABÉU

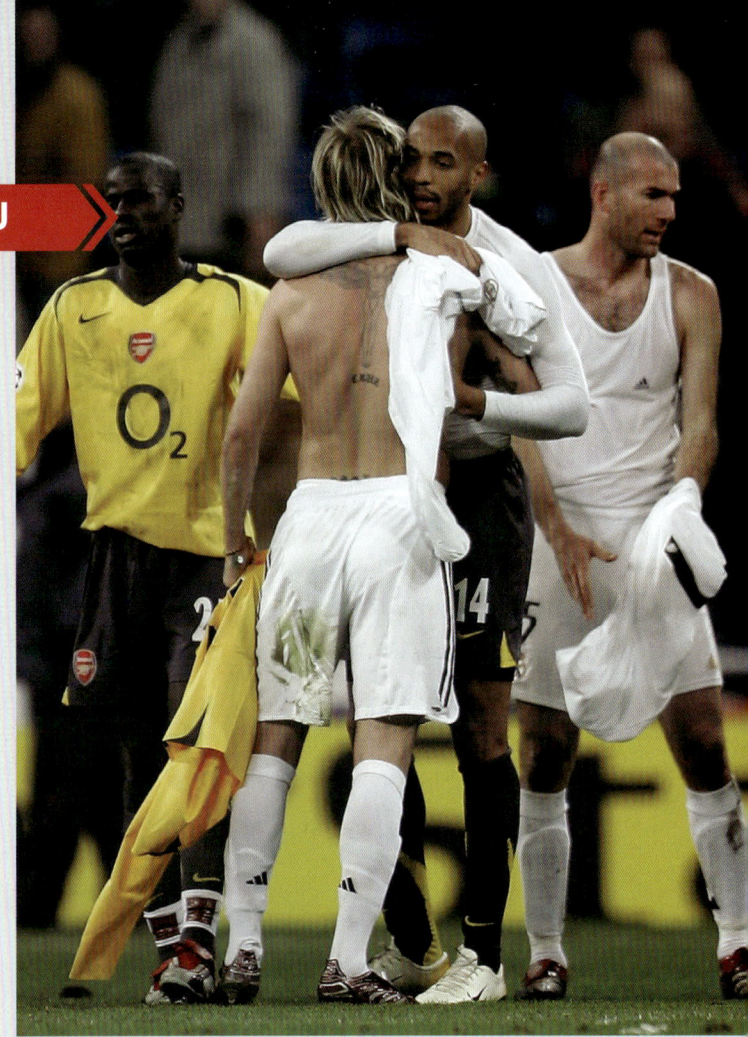

The 2005-06 Champions League adventure saw the Gunners proceed all the way to the final. Along the way came some famous victories, but none were more savoured than the victory over European giants Real Madrid in the legendary Bernabéu stadium.

Real Madrid are synonymous with the European Cup; they feel they own the trophy and never give it up without a fight. Travelling to Madrid in February 2006 for a do-or-die last-16 second leg tie after a 0-0 draw at Highbury was never going to be easy. Understandably then, Arsenal fans expectations were tempered when they saw their injury-depleted team and makeshift defence line-up at the Bernabéu against the likes of David Beckham, Zinidine Zidane, Roberto Carlos and Ronaldo.

And yet, as soon as the match kicked-off, Arsenal shook off the poor form that had derailed their league season. For nearly half-an-hour they dominated the game. José Antonio Reyes shot in the opening minutes was well saved by Casillas, only a desperate Carlos tackle denied Freddie Ljungburg and Thierry Henry sent a header wide when it looked easier to score. The visitors were well organised with Gilbert protecting the back four and 18-year-old Cesc Fàbregas and Ljungberg controlling the midfield. Only in the latter stages of the half did Real Madrid stir as Beckham sent a header just wide and then was foiled by Jens Lehmann at the edge of the area.

The visitors had real confidence going into the second half and it proved well founded. Thierry Henry's 34th Champions League goal came just two minutes after the break and it was a beauty. Picking up a pass from Fàbregas in the centre circle he surged into the Madrid half, skipping passed challenges from three defenders. Now 12-yards out with Sergio Ramos about to slide across his path, the striker calmly stroked an angled shot into the far corner of the net.

▲ David Beckham gets a consolatory hug from Thierry Henry after Arsenal's historic win at the Bernabéu

Real roused themselves in attempt to strike back, but Lehmann and his defence were in no mood to give anything away. Indeed while they fired crosses over in vain, the best chances fell to Ljungberg and substitute Abou Diaby. It was a victory built on resolve and skill from a team given little chance and a moment in history. They had become the first English team to beat Real Madrid at the renowned Santiago Bernabéu Stadium.

Competition: Champions League
Teams: Real Madrid vs Arsenal
Date: 21 February 2006
Venue: Santiago Bernabéu Stadium, Madrid
Final score: Real Madrid 0-1 Arsenal

TOP 10 GREATEST GAMES OF ALL TIME

ARSENAL

TONY
ADAMS